The
SUCCESS
GUIDE
to
BIPOLAR
DISORDER

Published by Advantage, Charleston, South Carolina.
Member of Advantage Media Group.

ADVANTAGE is a registered trademark and the Advantage colophon is a trademark of Advantage Media Group, Inc.

Printed in the United States of America.

ISBN: 978-1-59932-053-3
LCCN: 2007937133

Most Advantage Media Group titles are available at special quantity discounts for bulk purchases for sales promotions, premiums, fundraising, and educational use. Special versions or book excerpts can also be created to fit specific needs.

For more information, please write: Special Markets, Advantage Media Group, P.O. Box 272, Charleston, SC 29402 or call 1.866.775.1696.

The SUCCESS GUIDE to BIPOLAR DISORDER

Scot Ferrell
with Patricia Scott

Advantage™

CONTENTS

ACKNOWLEDGEMENTS

To my girlfriend, Patricia: without you, this book would have never been written. Thank you for loving, supporting and believing in me.

To Blue and GFunk: I'm grateful to God that you're both in my life.

To Teresa: God brought you into my life and I will forever be blessed because you loved me.

To Aunt Frances: You've always been the one I could call "Mom". Thank you for protecting and loving me.

To Talmadge, Jeannine, LaClita, Milton, and Dwight: You're a special family. Thanks for showing me how a family can love each other.

To Cathy and Bethie: You were there when no one else wanted to be. I love you both.

To Theresa Frady: You've known me since high school and you still love me!

To LeeAnn Headley: My grateful appreciation to you and God for our Christ-ordained friendship.

To Robby Murray: You have not, nor will you ever, be forgotten.

To Michael Johnson: You are my hero.

To Meg, Casey, Beth, Julie, Kendrick, Lasanna, O.C., Des, John Robert, Ryan, Chris, Matt, Jack, Charley, Jeremy, Josh, Dustin, Critter, Stephen, Weston, B.J., Matt, Todd, Thomas, and Caleb: Thank you for allowing me to be your coach.

To Steve Propst: You were an inspiration to me when I didn't believe it was possible to win.

To Mr. Beverly Clayton: You taught me so much more than chemistry and physics. Thank you!

To Kim Mankin: Thank you for the support through the years.

To Art, Doug, Lowery, Marty and Michael: Thank you for being such great mentors to me!

To Dr. Christine Gustafson: Thank you for helping me to find additional success strategies to speed my journey down the road to a life lived without medication.

To Dr. Marion Maloof: Thank you for giving me the tools to help my body heal itself and more importantly, the gift of your friendship.

To Dr. Kenneth Sobel: Thank you for saving my life so many years ago. I'm glad you didn't give up on me!

To Dr. Randy Kennedy: You will find your own words throughout this whole book. Thank you for believing in me and this project, praying for me, loving me and being my pastor.

To Gary Burley: Thank you for being my mentor and friend.

To Amanda, Hannah, Marissa, Nathan, Chris, Thomas, Felix, Michael, Aaron, Mark, A.J., David, Josh, Rocco, Hugo and Jeffrey (aka "Ricky Bobby"): Even though I give you a hard time, I want you to know that you've blessed my life!

To Landis, Zambo, Drake, Cromie, Hawley, Neace, Grant, Free, Schroer, Ranus, Smith, Patterson, Avery, Harris, Peek, White, Mason, Mangino, Rea, McMillian, Knight, Archibald, Braschler, Gardner, Maloney, Tolbert, and Dowse: Thank you for the support and the friendship.

To the Atlanta Northpoint Mall Mens' Wearhouse Gang: Albert, Angelo, Bobby, Larry, Terri, and Crystal: Thanks for helping me dress for success!

To Tammi, Cookie, and others who have lost someone to bipolar disorder: Through our pain, we reach out to others.

INTRODUCTION

> *"How vain is it to sit down to write when you have not stood up to live."*
>
> —Henry David Thoreau

WHY I COULD HAVE QUIT

Here are all of the reasons why I could have given up when things looked the darkest:

- I was the child of two alcoholic parents, one of whom had bipolar disorder.

- I was sexually abused in my early teens.

- Some of my closest teenage friends, to this day, remain in jail or are now dead.

- I was diagnosed with bipolar disorder in 1995.

- I was also diagnosed with a reading and writing disability in 1995.

- I was an alcoholic who used drugs regularly during my teen and early adult years.

- I was divorced in my thirties due to difficulties arising from my bipolar disorder.

- I had lost several hundred thousand dollars by the age of forty.

- I was accidentally overdosed twice on prescription medications.

I am a mentor, not a counselor or a doctor. I am a mentor to people because I have lived the "bipolar life"—the endless rounds of ineffective medication, the horrible side effects, and the loss of identity, career, money, and treasured relationships.

If you have been diagnosed with bipolar disorder, or if you have loved someone with bipolar disorder, you may have sought out other information about your illness. This book is different from any other book you may have read regarding this disorder. It will teach you how to **overcome** bipolar disorder using the proven process I have discovered through my own painful and exhilarating experiences. This book will unlock the magic within you to successfully win the battle against bipolar disorder, to live your greatest dreams and to give you hope for a bright future.

Now, I'll share with you what I've won:

- I have lived for four years episode- and symptom-free.

- I rose above my reading and writing disorder to graduate cum laude from college and to author several books.

- I founded and am the chairman of a non-profit foundation that educates pastors, the public, and the business world about psychological disorders and their successful management.

- One of my personal passions is to mentor clients in the management of their psychological disorders by utilizing the success strategies I discovered to manage my own bipolar disorder. This book is a passionate outreach.

- I have stable finances and own another company through which I speak and author articles, books, and audio products about successful psychological disorder management. In addition, I mentor and speak to athletes and those in religious and corporate organizations about creating a "will to win" attitude.

- My life is richly blessed with the loving and warm relationships of friends and family.

- I am fulfilled in every sense of the word—personally and professionally—with joy, health, and wealth.

One of my passions in life is to share my process with you so that you can begin to change your life today, this minute, for the better. So begin reading and be prepared to change your life from this moment on...so you, too, can discover that **victory is your only option!**

CHAPTER 1
What Do You Want?

> *"If you take too long in deciding what to do with your life, you'll find you've done it."*
>
> —George Bernard Shaw

WHAT DO YOU WANT?

What do you want? No, really, what do you want? I'm being serious. What do you really want? I guess you're wondering why I've asked this question three times. It seems to arouse more emotional reactions than any other question I ask my clients. It's the most important question I can ask them and the most difficult for them to answer. Most people are never asked what they really want in life, so they continue doing day by day what someone else expects of them. Normally, they are following a dream that is not their own. Perhaps long ago you traded in your dreams for someone else's because what you really wanted seemed unattainable.

DREAM AGAIN

Before you answer this question, allow me to take you back to the days when dreams flowed freely through your mind. For most of us, this was during our childhood—before so many people with good intentions told us to wake up and face the real world. When you're a kid, your life has no limits and you can sit for hours imagining all the things you'll do when you get older. Your thoughts are filled with all the colors of the spectrum, glittering with hope and promise as you explore the wonders of the world.

When I was a kid, I wanted to be Batman. I was a comic book junkie, and with each new issue, my triumphs as the Black Knight grew. With each page I turned, I was transported further and further away from my own life and was absorbed into the darkness of the world that was Batman. I wrapped myself in a black cape, vengeance seeping from my veins, blending with the shadows and smelling the fear and terror rising from the streets below. The feeling of invincibility rushed through my blood as I chased the Joker, Penguin, and the Riddler, mercilessly decimating their crews.

I was well armed for destruction. I carried my weapons of choice around my waist—a boomerang, sleeping gas, antidotes, levitation devices, remote control, and sonar devices. The blackness of the Batmobile foreshadowed the pain I inflicted as the night progressed. I felt the adrenaline rush as I punched the accelerator to the floor and sped out of the Bat Cave, riding into the night. Merging with the shadows, the air shimmered with panic as the city's vermin sensed my presence. Their flesh crawled and hysteria loomed as I stood before them, judge or executioner. Vengeance or Justice. Which way would the pendulum swing?

My persona of Batman was my way of escaping a very painful childhood. My dreams kept me alive and sane and helped to usher me to the age when I could change my circumstances. The ability to change my circumstances saved my life.

Your dreams may be very different from mine, and more than likely so. But whatever your dreams, let's return to them.

Right now, I want you to stop reading, close your eyes, and take yourself back to the time when you could dream of fantasy and victory. Take yourself back to the place where there were no limitations and the only thing that could stop you was your own imagination.

Now let all the cares of the world slide off your shoulders. Feel your body becoming more and more relaxed. Your whole being becomes still. Focus your attention on your breathing. Imagine yourself in a place where time doesn't exist and you have endless amounts of fantasies filled with thrilling and exciting outcomes. Breathe deeply and feel in your soul a sense of relaxation. Visualize a place where teachers, parents, employers, spouses, loved ones, boundaries, limits, money problems, and bipolar disorder do not exist.

Dream.

Let go of reality. Let your mind wander without limits. Now that you've reached the place where you can safely dream, what are you dreaming of?

Is it a passion-filled relationship, candlelight dinners, long, hot, wet, slow kisses, and chill bumps each time the person touches you?

Is it writing the world's next Alfred Hitchcock movie script?

Is it quitting your job and going into full-time ministry?

Is it living a symptom-free life and enjoying the pleasure of never seeing the inside of a psychiatrist's office again?

Dreams are emotion based. They're filled with passion. You may be sitting and dreaming about a symptom-free life, but in your current reality, there seems to be no way to achieve that dream. This is the mysterious power of dreaming that so few understand. Dreams are God-given gifts of passion. They're filled with magic and mystery.

Let me give you an example of what dreams really are. I recently asked my girlfriend, who worked in corporate America at the time, what her dream was. She talked about getting certain sales accounts, making a specific amount of money, and maintaining a stable position in her company. None of these, I pointed out, were her dreams; rather they were her goals. Again, I asked her, "What is your dream?" After a few moments, she said to me that her dream was to be happy. Even then, she still could not define what happiness meant to her. Then she finally looked at me and said, "I don't have any dreams now...they died a long time ago."

I hear this all the time. Most peoples' dreams died when they were teenagers. Has anyone ever said to you, "You need to give up XXXX (fill in the blank). One of these days, you're going to have to get a real job"? People say they want happiness but can't define what it actually is or what it means to them. They have ideas but have given up because they think their dreams are unattainable. They're no longer able to dream. The magic is gone, the glitter has faded, and they're left with the passionless vacuum of a life. We have lost the magic, the wonder, and the joy of a Christmas morning after Santa has come, or the goose bumps from our first kiss.

Because most adults experience the "loss of childhood innocence," people who are diagnosed with bipolar disorder experience a dual loss—the loss of innocence combined with the loss of their dreams. Diagnosed individuals are repeatedly told by the medical community that the life they once dreamed of is unattainable because of their illness. The feelings of hope, promise and future happiness are destroyed.

But these are exactly the feelings I want you to have again.

Do not let the illness take away the life you've dreamed about and wanted so badly. I give you permission to take every self-defeating thought, every limitation that has been placed upon you by doctors and loved ones, and make them vanish as if you had a magic wand. They will disappear when you begin to dream again.

Now, I ask you again: what do you really want?

Before you answer, you may want to know what I really wanted. I wanted it all: a symptom-free life, a hot, flashy sports car, a meaningful career that I loved and that provided me with the chance to help children and adults overcome their own obstacles, the financial abundance that would reward my entrepreneurial efforts, the house of my dreams, and someone I could love with all my heart who would love me unconditionally even with my illness. In my deepest dreams, I wanted to be loved. I knew that I could achieve all of the other dreams, but I always worried that I would never find the love I dreamed of so passionately.

Fast forward my life to today. Next week, I'll test-drive a new luxury SUV, and a sports car. I just fixed my girlfriend a candlelit dinner. We plan on getting married next year and we're shopping for the house of our dreams. The company I started last year is beginning to take off, I'm the founder and chairman of a charitable foundation that helps people with psychological disorders, and I've been symptom-free for almost five years now.

It's time to take off the gloves and fight to regain your dreams. So I ask you for the final time…

What do *you* want?

Success Summary

- Learn to dream again.

- Identify what you really want.

- Write down what you really want.

CHAPTER 2
Attitude and Acceptance

> *We can alter our lives by altering our attitudes of mind.*
>
> —William James

WHY IS ATTITUDE SO IMPORTANT?

> *If your ship doesn't come in, swim out to it.*
>
> —Jonathan Winters

Attitude is so important because it is the one factor that will decide victory or failure in every area of your life. Your attitude is the one thing that you control, every second, every minute, every hour of every day. Your attitude affects:

- your belief in your potential for your success

- your perception and reaction to a challenge

- your confidence in yourself and your ability to change

- your perception and reaction to an opportunity

YOUR ATTITUDE

> *Believe in yourself! Have faith in your abilities! Without a humble but reasonable confidence in your own powers, you cannot be successful or happy.*
>
> —Norman Vincent Peale

Right now is a good time to check your attitudes toward life and your illness. Write out the answers to the following questions:

1) Do I constantly think about what I "coulda/woulda/shoulda" done with my life?

2) Do I have problems taking responsibility for my actions?

3) Do I have difficulties accepting feedback?

4) Who do I feel is responsible for improving my life?

5) Do I see problems as opportunities or obstacles?

6) Am I grateful for each day?

7) Do I have the courage to sit down with my loved ones and ask them in a non-emotional conversation, "How do I treat you?

8) Am I open to managing my illness through means other than medication?

9) Do I have an emergency plan in place in case something does happen?

10) Am I happy with the quality of my life right now?

Now analyze your answers.

Do you wonder where these answers came from or why you answered the way you did? In order to change your attitude, you need to understand how you came to embrace the attitudes that you currently have. The following will help you understand why you answered the questions the way you did.

ORIGIN OF ATTITUDES

You can never plan for the future by the past.

—Edmund Burke

Wherever you go, you are bombarded by positive and negative images and information from your past and present. Of course, whatever constantly surrounds you on a day-to-day basis automatically becomes programmed into your thinking and beliefs without you realizing it. All of us have experienced this type of programming since we were little children.

Although it helps if you had positive and supportive parents, the fact is that most of us had average parents who inadvertently passed on to us the same limiting beliefs and negative programming they grew up with. But remember, the past is the past. There is no payoff for blaming your parents for your current level of self-confidence. It's now your responsibility to take charge of your own self concept and your beliefs. You must choose to believe that you can do anything you set your mind to—anything—because, in fact, you can. It might help you to know that the latest brain research now indicates that with enough positive self-talk and positive visualization, combined with the proper training, coaching and practice, anyone can learn to do almost anything.

NEGATIVE PROGRAMMING

Negative programming, I feel, is one of the most insidious factors that pervades our culture today. Many of us as children heard things like these:

- You're not smart enough, pretty enough, thin enough, tall enough, the right race, etc.

- You could never do that, that's a crazy idea—it will never work....

- Why can't you be more like your brother?

- If you were "normal," we wouldn't have these problems.

On and on it goes until we become programmed and we don't even realize it. The worst part about this whole process is that most of the things that we were told were said by those who loved us the most—our first grade teachers, our parents, brothers and sisters, grandparents, piano teachers and coaches, all well-meaning adults. Most of us never realize that a majority of our daily decisions are an outcome of our programming. It's no wonder why some of us have such a negative attitude toward having an illness like bipolar disorder. If your attitude was negative before you were diagnosed, why do you expect to have a great attitude after your diagnosis?

POSITIVE PROGRAMMING

On the flip side, some people are inundated with messages of support and strength. Just like the children who experienced negative programming, some kids heard things like this:

- That was a great job on your report card!

- You can be and achieve anything you want.

- Always follow your dreams.

- Mistakes are how we learn.

- All I ask is that you do your best.

The funny thing is that the same people who make the negative comments are also the same ones who make the positive comments— the teachers, the parents, the siblings, the coaches, etc. Your job is to identify if you've been programmed with positive or negative ideas. The beginning of the healing process is to know yourself so you can build upon your strengths.

YOUR VIEWS ON DIAGNOSIS

Attitude dramatically affects those first critical days and months after *the diagnosis*. Your attitude pre-diagnosis will generally determine which of the following categories you'll be in post-diagnosis. See if you can find yourself in one of the three following categories of diagnosis acceptance:

- denial

- over-identification with the illness

- solution-oriented focus

Denial

Throughout the last several years, I have met with so many people who absolutely refuse to acknowledge their illness. They fear/feel that if they acknowledge the symptoms or the diagnosis, they will be forced to choose or refuse to accept responsibility for the management of their illness and the consequences of their actions. Here is what I hear repeatedly:

- My wife's the moody one, not me.

- My husband doesn't understand me.

- I'm not sick...I really *am* the last prophet.

- Why do I need to take medicine? There's nothing wrong with me.

- Everyone is out to get me.

- My spouse is just oversensitive to the things I say and do.

- It (extramarital relationships) doesn't mean anything...I just have a high sex drive.

- This is just the way I am. It is what it is. I'm never going to change.

I've watched this kind of reasoning destroy many lives. These people usually lose their houses, jobs, spouses, children and everything they've worked for most of their lives. The sad thing is that after all of this has happened, they *still* refuse to acknowledge that there is a problem.

Many times, I end up meeting with their loved ones because they are frustrated their efforts have met with little results. Sadly, I have to tell these loved ones that I cannot help them because the person that has the illness is in total denial. **Until you embrace personal responsibility and act accordingly, you will never find a successful victory over bipolar disorder.**

Over-Identification

> *Self-pity is our worst enemy and if we yield to it,*
> *we can never do anything good in the world.*
> *Although the world is full of suffering, it*
> *is full also of the overcoming of it.*
>
> —Helen Keller

This category would be as bad as denial except for one factor: these people have actually admitted that they have an illness. They usually take on the mantle of "the victim" and will wear it proudly. They act as if they are helpless to do anything to control the illness. Read the following list and see if you can identify with any of these statements:

- I only scream at my children because I have bipolar disorder.

- Late night shopping channels are only designed to exploit people who have bipolar disorder.

- I'm too sick to get a job.

- The government *should* take care of me—I have a debilitating illness!

- My family members have to understand that I have an illness, and *they* need to adjust to my moods.

- One day, they'll have a pill that will fix all of my problems.

- Affairs happen when you have bipolar disorder.

- I can't help that I spend so much money. I have bipolar disorder.

These individuals seem to be able to blame every single circumstance in their lives on their illness. Life has dealt them a bad hand, and they embrace having no control over any of life's events. I do not accept these people as my clients. There's one big reason why people like this irritate me to no end: I was one of them, once upon a time. I blamed every single thing I did on the fact I had bipolar disorder. I expected every person in my life to accept my mood swings without question and deal with the fact that I could be an ass any time I wanted to be. They were the ones who needed to change, not me.

Eventually, I was so tired of listening to the nonsense I was saying, I wanted to kick myself in my own ass. I was a long-suffering victim until one day in my general practitioner's office, life changed forever. I was doing my normal whining and complaining to him when he stopped me in mid-sentence and said, "Stop being such a baby (he used much stronger words than this) and get over it. People are diagnosed with illnesses every day. Why should you be any different? It's about time you accepted some responsibility and took control of your life."

From that day forward, I took his advice and changed my outlook on life.

Solution-Oriented Focus

Solution-oriented people accept the diagnosis once they have received second opinions and set a course to understand the illness and find *effective* treatments. These people realize that changes must be made in their nutritional intake, daily routine, exercise, attitude, behavior management and supplementation. They realize that a psychological disorder is *no different* from any other illness and that a proactive approach is needed in order to be successful. I am proud to say I now fit into this category and have for many years. Some people reading this book won't need to change their attitudes (but keep reading anyway—I've got some great tips for quality living for you!)

Now that you have identified which category you are in, and how your attitude toward your illness was shaped, *how do you fix it?*

HOW DO YOU FIX IT?

The future is purchased by the present.

—Dr. Samuel Johnson

Attitudes operate on three planes:

- thought

- speech

- behavior

The man who acquires the ability to take full possession of his own mind may take possession of anything else to which he is justly entitled.

—Andrew Carnegie

It's true…you are what you think. Thoughts become things! Thoughts are magnetic, and thoughts have a frequency. As you think thoughts, they are sent out into the Universe, and they magnetically attract like things operating on the same frequency. Everything sent out returns to the source—you. You are like a human transmission tower, transmitting a frequency with your thoughts. If you want to change anything in your life, change the frequency by changing your thoughts.

You have to be able to control your thought patterns if you want to control your attitude. If you constantly think about negative things, negative things will constantly happen to you. But if you *focus with feeling* on the positives of life, you will be amazed at how many positive things come your way.

Remember that your thoughts are the primary cause of everything. When you think a sustained thought, it is immediately sent out into the Universe. That thought magnetically attaches itself to the like or similar frequency, and the within seconds sends the reading of that frequency back to you through your feelings. To restate, your feelings are a communication back to you from the Universe, telling you what frequency you are currently on. Your feelings become your frequency feedback mechanism.

When you are feeling good feelings, it is a communication back from the Universe saying, "You are thinking good thoughts." Likewise, when you are feeling bad, you are receiving communication back from the Universe saying, "You are thinking bad thoughts."

So when you are feeling bad, in effect the Universe is saying, "Warning! Change your thinking now. Negative frequency recording. Change frequency. Counting down to manifestation. Warning!"

The next time you are feeling bad or feeling any negative emotion, listen to the signal you are receiving from the Universe. In that moment, you are blocking your own good from coming to you because you are on a negative frequency. Change your thoughts and think about something good, and when the good feelings start to come, you will know it was because you shifted yourself onto a new frequency, and the Universe has confirmed it with better feelings.

To quote Bob Doyle, author and Law of Attraction specialist, "You're getting exactly what you're feeling about, not so much what you're thinking about. That's why people tend to spiral if they stub their toe getting out of bed. Their whole day goes like that. They have no clue that a simple shifting of their emotions can change their entire day—and life. If you start out having a good day and you're in that particular happy feeling, as long as you don't allow something to change your mood, you're going to continue to attract, by the law of attraction, more situations and people that sustain that happy feeling."

You can shift your thoughts to what you want and receive confirmation through your feelings that you changed your frequency, and the law of attraction will grab hold of that new frequency and send it back to you as the new pictures of your life.

The first step is to be aware of your thoughts. If you catch yourself thinking negative thoughts, use the following table to help you transform them into positive ones.

Negative Thoughts	Replace With These Positive Thoughts
I'm afraid…	I can if I want to badly enough…
I can't…	I can face any challenge…
I should've…	I'm doing the best I can…
Why me?	Why not me?
What if my whole day tomorrow is terrible?	What if my whole day tomorrow is wonderful?

We're not talking positive affirmations, here. We are talking about attaching emotions and feelings to positive thoughts—it's called visualization.

Here's a very powerful story about visualization. It's a quotation from Morris Goodman, better known as The Miracle Man.

"My story begins on March 10, 1981. This day really changed my whole life. It was a day I'll never forget. I crashed an airplane. I ended up in the hospital completely paralyzed. My spinal cord was crushed, I broke the first and second cervical vertebrae, my swallowing reflex was destroyed, I couldn't eat or drink, my diaphragm was destroyed, I couldn't breathe. All I could do was blink my eyes. The doctors, of course, said I'd be a vegetable the rest of my life. All I'd be able to do is blink my eyes. That's the picture they saw of me, but it didn't matter what they thought. The main thing was what I thought. I pictured myself being a normal person again, walking out of that hospital.

"The only thing I had to work with in the hospital was my mind, and once you have your mind, you can put things back together again.

"I was hooked to a respirator and they said I'd never breathe on my own again because my diaphragm was destroyed. But a little voice kept saying to me, 'Breathe deeply, breathe deeply.' And finally I was weaned from it. They were at a loss for an explanation. I could not afford to allow anything to come into my mind that would distract me from my goal or from my vision.

"I had set a goal to walk out of the hospital on Christmas. And I did. I walked out the hospital on my own two feet. They said it couldn't be done. That's a day I will never forget.

"For people who are sitting out there right now and are hurting, if I wanted to sum up my life and sum up for people what they can do in life, I would sum it up in six words: 'Man becomes what he thinks about.'" (Excerpt from *The Secret* by Rhonda Byrne)

Today, Morris Goodman is an author and international speaker who travels the world inspiring others.

For a more "everyday" example of visualization, consider this: my girlfriend *really* wants to purchase a convertible sports car. So, to help her focus on bringing that positive *thing* to her (remember, thoughts become things), she produces positive thoughts by several different methods. She has picture of the car she wants posted in her office where she sees it all the time. She made a "visualization playlist" for her iPod filled with upbeat "driving music" so she can visualize how happy she will be when she gets the car and can drive down the road with the wind blowing through her hair, singing the songs she already downloaded onto her iPod. **So, before she ever gets the car, she has already experienced the positive emotions that the car will bring her through visualization.**

The funny thing is, she is already happier…even without the car. Just the exercise of visualizing with emotion and feeling has charged her attitude with the energy of positive thoughts, and those positive thoughts will bring her the car of her dreams. Thoughts…become…things.

> *Change your thoughts and you change your world.*
>
> —Norman Vincent Peale

Speech

Have you ever replayed what you said throughout the day? How often did you use negative words? For most people, negative words and phrases are an ingrained part of daily conversation. Are the following phrases parts of your everyday vocabulary?

- I hate…

- I'll just die if that happens!

- I can't afford that!

- I just can't because…

- Life's a bitch and then you die.

- Some people are just lucky…

- I deserve that more than he does.

- I am so stressed out!

- It's not my fault!

- My children drive me nuts!

Do any of these remind you of someone, or did reading these make you think of several negative things *you* say on a daily basis? Now, just think about how each word you say shapes the outcome of your day. What would happen if you replaced all the negatives with positives? Do you think your life would improve? Here, let me save you the trouble of answering that question. Science has already proven that this is a fact! Try these!

- I choose not to purchase that right now.

- I will find a way to…

- I can because…

- I'm very busy…isn't that a great problem to have?

- I'm happy for Jim. He worked hard to get that promotion.

- Luck always follows hard work.

- It's my responsibility.

- My children are a blessing!

Tomorrow, set aside twenty-four hours and use only positive words and phrases. You will be amazed at how much better you feel, how people react to you, and how positive you feel about the future. But remember, you must do this with *feeling*!

> *It is the way we react to circumstances that determines our feelings.*
>
> —Dale Carnegie

Behavior

Everyone reacts differently to every situation. Stressful situations and the way you react to them tend to show what kind of a person you really are. You have to realize that you are *always* responsible for your actions and how you treat other people. Having bipolar disorder *does not* give you a free license to be rude to people, yell at your spouse or children, have extramarital affairs, bankrupt your family's savings, quit job after job, be totally irresponsible or refuse to take a proactive role in the treatment of your illness. Controlling your thoughts and speech *must* be backed up by positive behaviors. Here's several suggestions on how to change your behaviors to match your positive thoughts and speech:

- Establish a routine for your life.

- Monitor your thoughts for thinking patterns that produce "bad feelings."

- Replace bad habits (drinking, smoking, dismal eating habits, too much caffeine and poor sleep habits) with new positive behaviors such as a proper eating program, daily exercise, meditation, setting a sleep schedule, acquiring a hobby that accentuates the positive aspects of your illness, etc.

- Take time out of each day to be grateful for the positive things in your life.

- Take responsibility for what happens in your life instead of blaming other people or circumstances.

- Be proactive and aggressive in seeking and securing a successful treatment plan that works for *you* and is tailored to your biochemistry and desires.

- Visualize the positive things you want to happen in your life—make them real to you in any way possible! Feel the thoughts, don't just think them!

The Benefits of a Changed Attitude

We are what we repeatedly do; excellence, then, is not an act, but a habit.

—Aristotle

- increased enthusiasm

- freedom from the limitations of fear

- increased creativity

- exciting joy when using more of your God-given potential

- boundless opportunities

- increased efficiency in utilizing your time and energy

- enjoyment in taking the initiative…it's called *empowerment*

- abundance of positive friends and colleagues

- meaningful, intimate relationships

Now, doesn't life seem a lot more fun with a positive attitude? You have to realize that the only person that can stop you from having a wonderful life is you!

As an illustration, think about the following two guys whose lives changed because of their own attitude adjustments: Ebenezer Scrooge from *A Christmas Carol* and George Bailey from *It's a Wonderful Life*.

Ebenezer Scrooge began his life as most of us do: experiencing good times and bad, loneliness and happiness, and living with positive and negative role models. However, Ebeneezer began to obsess about money and it began to rule his life. This obsession colored his relationships and his personal habits, so much so that he was visited on Christmas Eve by three ghosts—the ghosts of Christmas past (happy times), Christmas present (not-so-happy times) and Christmas future (really unhappy times, i.e. Scrooge sees his own body in his grave with no one there to mourn his passing). He changes his tune and starts to enjoy life giving generously instead of being miserable as a miser. He realizes that life is to be appreciated, lived and enjoyed instead of being endured. Ebenezer was forced to realize that relationships are the important cog in the wheel of life.

George Bailey begins his life full of hope and dreams of traveling the world and blowing off his little one-horse hometown. But on the night of his scheduled departure to see the world, his father dies and George is left to take over the family business. He manages the business while his brother attends college with the understanding that his brother will return and allow George to travel. Yet again, George's dreams of world travel are thwarted when war breaks out and his brother leaves to fight in Europe. George is left to mind the store as his brother becomes a war hero, saving hundreds of lives. Finally, George marries his long-time sweetheart and as they leave town to honeymoon in exotic places, economic hardship hits and George must use all of his personal cash to save the family business. Frustrated beyond belief, George is then accused of financial theft when one of his family members who works in the business loses the receipts from the daily intake of cash. George staggers onto a bridge in the middle of a snowstorm, despondent and depressed, and plans to jump in the river to commit suicide when he sees another man jump into the river ahead of him. Unknown to George, he rescues an angel named Clarence who has been sent to show George what a wonderful life he really has.

Both Ebeneezer and George had a revelation about how they were living their lives and got a "second chance" to change things for the better. I hope this book is the revelation you need to seize your second chance! Don't worry, I won't be sending the ghosts of Bipolar Past, Present and Future to your house! If they show up, it's your own fault!

It's never too late…you're never too old. If I can do it, you can, too.

Success Summary

- Your attitude determines victory or failure.

- Positive or negative programming determines your initial attitudes toward life.

- There are three categories of diagnosis acceptance: denial, over-identification and solution-oriented focus.

- Attitude operates on three planes: thought, speech, and behavior.

- The benefits of a changed attitude include enthusiasm, freedom, opportunities, increased energy, empowerment, joy and meaningful relationships.

I can't wait for success...so I went ahead without it.

—Jonathan Winters

CHAPTER 3
Doctors and Medication

*The doctor of the future will give no medicine,
but will interest his or her patients in the care
of the human frame, and a proper diet, and
in the cause and prevention of disease.*

—Thomas A. Edison

A DISCLAIMER

Before I start this section, I want everyone reading this book to understand the following: I fully realize that there *are* good doctors who serve their patients well. Some of them are my closest friends. I have been fortunate enough to have sourced some exceptional doctors to be on my "treatment team." I have a physician that specializes in integrative medicine and a psychiatrist that works with me on a team basis exchanging ideas and strategies to ensure optimal treatment results. The most crucial member of my team is my doctor, who practices integrative medicine and monitors my neurotransmitter, vitamin, mineral, hormone and thyroid levels. Integrative medicine combines treatments from conventional medicine with proven, safe and effective complementary and alternative treatments. Integrative medicine is practiced by board certified doctors.

In defense of most doctors, they receive very little education in any treatments other than pharmacology and surgery. They design treatment plans for patients based on what they currently know. With the overwhelming demands of managed care and backbreaking patient loads, many doctors simply do not have time to keep up with current research outside of pharmacology or surgery. Add to that the pressure of the increasing numbers of physicians who are leaving the medical fields, again due to the frustrations of rising malpractice insurance costs, managed care and overwork. Fewer and fewer students are enrolling in psychiatry and in medical school in general. The liability of the medical practice is simply becoming too much for some doctors to manage. All of this leads to our current state of affairs in psychiatry.

I would like to state clearly that I am not a medical doctor and have no medical degrees of any type nor do I plan to attend medical school anytime in the future. Any information offered in this section is my opinion. I have obtained information for my personal action plan through endless amounts of research, and I'll be sharing the results of that research with you in this section. I am not licensed to create "treatment plans."

After twelve years of therapy my psychiatrist said something that brought tears to my eyes. He said, "No hablo ingles."

—Ronnie Shakes

As I look back over the last twelve years and consider all the feelings I've experienced towards doctors and medication, the list of emotions wouldn't be positive ones—frustration, irritation, anger, hopelessness, despair, rage, hatred, fury and numbness to name a few. With each doctor that treated me, the solution of how to manage bipolar disorder successfully became more evasive and unclear. Each doctor normally spent about two minutes actually listening to me before writing out prescriptions. The only answer they ever had to offer me was, "Take this pill, and if this one makes you feel bad, then we'll give you another one to make the effects of the first pill disappear." Does this sound crazy to anyone but me? At one time, I was on nine different medications, all of which were making me feel worse instead of better *and* producing new symptoms which I never even had before starting the medication. But the only answers I would get from the doctors would be, "All medications have side effects; you're going to be on them for the rest of your life and you'll just have to learn to live with it." Again, does this sound crazy to anyone but me?

I am a former high school special education teacher and basketball coach. At one time, the side effects from my medications were so bad that I forgot almost all the names of my students. I could not remember which classroom I taught in, and the vertigo was so bad I had to cling to the walls to walk down the school hallways. I have lost from my memory almost two years of the six that I taught at that high school. *Two years* of my life that I will never be able to get back. Just remembering it makes me feel rage all over again. Even though all of these symptoms and side effects were taking place, I still could not get one single doctor during this period to talk with me honestly and give me some straight answers. All anyone ever wanted to do was to give me another pill instead of trying to solve the problem.

Due to the ineffectiveness of my medications and the subsequent memory loss and the confusion they caused, I couldn't track my investments and assets and lost several hundred thousand dollars in the process. I also lost my home and eventually resigned from teaching. All because my doctors at the time would not listen to me when I talked about what the medications were doing to me, nor would they find a logical way to treat my illness. Now if that doesn't piss you off, I don't know what will. The only way I got through this horrible period was the fact that I realized I had to find an answer. Not just for me, but also for others out there who were going through the same experiences.

On top of everything, my doctor managed to give me an overdose of medication that caused me to have seizures and cost me two trips to the emergency room. Still to this day, I suffer residual aftereffects from this overdosing.

The final straw was when I went to the mental hospital and saw how psychiatric patients were treated. I was not mistreated, but I saw several other patients being treated less than humanely. At the hospital, most patients were heavily medicated and then were directed to go to "group therapy." I felt that group therapy was not effective because there were too many people in the session, most of whom had just been diagnosed and did not understand what was going on in their bodies or their lives. Some were too medicated to be clear about what was happening to them. My thoughts were at the time were "Why are we sitting around talking about our feelings when this is a biochemical illness and we should be looking for ways to correct our biochemical makeup?" When someone is diagnosed with diabetes, the doctor reviews step-by-step how the insulin levels will be corrected, not the patient's feelings regarding diabetes. **Why can't we do this with mental illness?** Your discussion of your feelings certainly has a place in the process, but it is not the first step. The first step is to find the root cause of what is causing your illness.

After going through all of this, about four years ago I decided to fight back. I finally realized I was acting like a "sheep" being led around by the psychiatric community and doing whatever they said to do, even though I wasn't experiencing any relief and my symptoms were actually getting worse using their treatment methods. Here I was, a successful basketball coach who for years had preached to his players that you make your own circumstances in life, that *anything* can be overcome with self-discipline and determination. I wasn't living *one thing* that I preached to my players.

I decided I could go back and apologize to every kid I had ever coached for lying to them, or I could finally go live the words I so often spoke. I chose to take control of the situation, and this book is one of the results of that decision. I'll cover my actual process later in this chapter.

CURRENT STATE OF AFFAIRS

We all (yes, even doctors) know that parts of the medical system are broken. However, rather than complain, I would like to offer some suggestions or alternative solutions for you to pursue or investigate on your own. Below are areas that I feel need to be addressed in order for you to receive adequate care in the future.

Current Process of Diagnosing

It has always frustrated me how diagnoses for most psychological disorders are made from behavior scales and charts, not from actual biochemical testing. If what doctors say is true, and our illness is truly a result of biochemical imbalances, why don't they just use a blood, urine or saliva test to check our neurotransmitter, vitamin/mineral, thyroid, hormone and heavy metal toxicity levels? Right now, doctors are only attacking symptoms, not the root causes of issues that might be the basis of our biochemical problems. Once many doctors make their "diagnosis," they begin writing prescriptions for symptoms, even though they have no idea what is actually causing the problems. This is the equivalent of taking your car to a mechanic and having him try to diagnose what is wrong with your car without ever looking at the engine, listening to the car run, talking to you about how the car is running or hooking the car up to a diagnostic computer to check the car's systems. Now be honest with yourself: how many of you would take your car to a mechanic who does business in this fashion? Can't you just see yourself pulling up to a garage as the mechanic walks out to your car, asks you how your car is feeling and then says to you, "Yeah, I think you've blown a head gasket," before turning around and walking back into the office? Of course, it sounds crazy to you to treat your car this way, so why do you line up month after month and allow doctors to do this to you?

Another thing that has always puzzled me about the diagnostic process is the relationship psychiatric hospitals have with patients. When an undiagnosed person is taken to a psychiatric hospital, immediately a questionnaire regarding the patient's behaviors is completed and a treatment plan is started. This plan normally includes medication being given to an *undiagnosed* patient. Standard hospital procedures in any non-psychiatric emergency room generally involve one or more of the following tests: blood, urine or saliva, X-rays, CAT scans, or MRIs, or EKG/EEG monitoring of some sort. No medication is dispensed (unless it is a life-threatening scenario) until the doctors produce evidence of a particular condition.

Let me clarify. I realize if someone is a danger to themselves or others that medication is sometimes the correct course of action. However, once a patient is stabilized, why aren't we doing medical testing to find the root causes of the problem? Instead, patients are instructed to continue to take medications for a diagnosis that was given without proper medical testing. It is no surprise that misdiagnosis is such a major issue in the psychiatric community. **No wonder it takes, on average, about eleven years to get an accurate diagnosis of bipolar disorder.** That's eleven years too long for someone to have to endure all that bipolar disorder brings with it.

Recently, a study conducted by a *medical association* showed that doctors give patients approximately fifteen seconds to make their point before they stop listening. Fifteen seconds. Even your car mechanic gives you more time than that to discuss your car's problems, and he stays focused on what you are saying when he is trying to diagnose it. He uses all your input, even the funny car sounds you make in order to identify where he needs to look first for problems. Then, he hooks the car up to the diagnostic computer to make a precise determination. There is *no guesswork* involved. However, in today's psychiatry, subjective interpretation is all that is used. This is no surprise to those in the psychiatric community who have been debating this issue for years.

One of the new, disturbing (I feel) diagnostic trends in psychiatry is for doctors to give out behavior scales to the educational community (i.e. teachers, counselors) to help in the overall diagnosis process. I'm a former special education teacher and I do not ever remember being asked to fill out a diagnostic form in order to help diagnose a child with cancer or diabetes. So why would the psychiatric community need a teacher's input to diagnose a biochemical disorder? I know that school counselors will respond with "But we have training in psychology." That may be true, but they have no medical training! Again, this goes back to this question: if this is an organically based illness, **why aren't we using real medical testing to diagnose an organically-based problem?**

DIAGNOSTIC SOLUTIONS

Now that we have discussed the problems with the diagnostic process, here are some areas that, if addressed, might render a more accurate and timely diagnosis.

Biochemical Testing—Neurotransmitters

Since most of psychiatric medicine focuses on the deficiency or abundance of neurotransmitter levels, we need to perform the proper neurotransmitter testing before any medicine of any type is administered (unless it is a crisis). Neurotransmitter testing is as simple as taking a blood, urine or saliva test. Once a doctor has a better understanding of your body's neurotransmitter functions, he or she can devise a treatment plan that will give you the optimal opportunity for successful management of your illness. On my "treatment team," my integrative medicine doctor is the one who performs this type of testing due to her in-depth knowledge of this topic.

Biochemical Testing—Thyroid

Many doctors already test their patients for thyroid performance. However, most use the THS blood test. To get a more accurate picture of thyroid activity, suggest that your doctor measure free T4, free T3, reverse T3, and possibly thyroid antibodies. Together, these are considered a complete battery of thyroid tests. The reason T3 is so important to measure is because it is a neurotransmitter that regulates the action of serotonin (the "feel good" hormone), norepinephrine, and gamma-aminobutyric (GABA). Norepinephrine, GABA, and their effects are listed on the neurotransmitter chart in Chapter 4.

Untreated thyroid problems can lead to some of the following symptoms:

- elevated cholesterol levels

- heart disease

- fatigue

- muscle weakness

- poor mental function

- depression

- weight gain

- risk of cancer

Biochemical Testing—Food Allergies

It is not uncommon for people in the United States to have food allergies due to all of the processed and chemically enhanced food we consume. This is an area of testing that many people simply overlook, and one that could be critical to your success. Common symptoms of food allergies are:

- upset stomach

- agitation

- anxiety

- irritability

- skin conditions

- hyperactivity

Biochemical Testing—Heavy Metal Toxicity

Due to environmental issues in the United States involving the water and air supplies, everyone is affected by some form of heavy metal toxicity. Your doctor can decide the appropriate tests for you. Here are some of the biggest concerns we face and their symptoms:

Arsenic

- abdominal pain

- diarrhea

- anorexia

- fever

- mucosal irritation

- arrhythmia

Lead

- mood swings

- convulsions

- hypertension

- renal dysfunction

- hallucinations

- vertigo

- fatigue

- sleeplessness

Mercury

- anxiety

- emotional instability

- fatigue

- cognitive and motor dysfunction

- insomnia

- tremors

- weakness

- forgetfulness

Cadmium

- learning disorders

- migraines

- growth impairment

- cardiovascular disease

- osteoporosis

- emphysema

- poor appetite

Aluminum

- Alzheimer's disease

- memory loss

- learning difficulty

- loss of coordination

- disorientation

- mental confusion

- headaches

Biochemical Testing—Vitamins and Minerals

In the United States, we live in a fast-food country, and most people are not getting the proper amounts of vitamins and minerals in their daily diet. Vitamins and minerals are imperative for proper physical and mental functioning. Don't think you can just go take a vitamin and everything in your body will be balanced. You need the proper testing and a personalized action plan; your integrative medicine doctor can do this for you. In Chapter 4 on nutrition, you will find some of the issues that can arise if you have deficiencies or imbalances of vitamins and minerals.

Biochemical Testing—Hormones

Many people just don't make the connection between hormones and physical and mental health. We see the physical signs of hormone imbalance before we see the mental symptoms. **Men, listen up...this is not just an area for my female readers! Hormones affect virtually every function in your body.** Without hormones, you cannot sleep, think clearly or maintain proper health; your weight goes out of control, your sexual ability and desire decreases, your eyesight diminishes and your body temperature becomes impossible to regulate—and on and on and on. Basically, without hormones, you die slowly, and it's not a pretty death.

Listed below are your body's hormones and their functions:

HORMONE	SITE OF PRODUCTION	FUNCTION
Estrogen (includes estradiol and estriol)	Ovaries, adrenal glands, fat cells, placenta (during pregnancy only)	Regulates a woman's passage through menstruation, fertility and menopause Supports the growth and regeneration of female reproductive tissues Develops secondary sex characteristics such as body hair, breasts and distribution of body fat Keeps the uterus, urinary tract, breasts and blood vessels toned and flexible
Progesterone	Ovaries, adrenal glands (women and men), testicles (men)	Regulates menstrual cycle Sustains a pregnancy Stimulates bone-building cells (osteoclasts) and increases the rate of new bone formation Promotes energy production in the brain Protects against nerve cell damage and brain aging

DHEA	Adrenal glands	Precursor (building block) to sex hormones Involved in sex drive Maintains collagen levels in the skin for promoting smoother, younger-looking skin Works as a integrative medicine antidote to negative effects of cortisol
Thyroid	Thyroid gland	Affects all metabolic activity Regulates temperature Regulates heart rate Increases fat breakdown Controls metabolism of carbohydrates and fat Lowers cholesterol Keeps hair, skin and nails healthy
Cortisol	Adrenal glands	Keeps us awake and alert Mobilizes sugar for energy
Adrenaline	Adrenal glands	Mobilizes sugar for energy Functions as an integrative medicine stimulant
Insulin	Pancreas	Determines whether fat will be burned or stored Involved in growth

Human Growth Hormone	Pituitary gland	Controls chronic inflammation Beneficial to organ systems, including the heart and brain Protects immunity Increases aerobic capacity Protects bone Regulates body composition by decreasing body fat and enhancing muscle tone Provides energy and endurance Lowers blood pressure Improves memory Improves vision Enhances ability to deal with stress Enhances sleep Responsible for growth
Melatonin	Pineal gland in the brain; small amounts in retina and gastrointestinal tract	Increases quality of sleep Is a potent antioxidant and captures damaging free radicals Activates thyroid hormones Improves mood and relieves anxiety Improves sleep disorders Fights the growth of cancer cells Improves immune system Relaxes muscles and relieves tension

TESTING SUMMARY

Due to the daily ingestion of toxins from our water and air supply and our nutritional intake, it is imperative that you discuss with your integrative medicine doctor about having these tests performed:

- neurotransmitter levels

- thyroid levels

- food allergies

- heavy metal toxicity levels

- vitamin/mineral levels

- hormone levels

When I had my tests performed, I was flabbergasted at how out of whack my biochemistry was. My integrative medicine doctor did a very thorough examination, conducted all needed testing and was able to immediately administer vitamin and mineral injections. She also pointed out that even though I was taking several vitamin and mineral supplements, my body was absorbing very little of what I was taking. Even though you think you are taking in all of the needed nutrients, a "leaky gut" can prevent your body from absorbing any of the nutrients you're putting into your body. From her exam and the test results, it was clear that a "leaky gut" was causing me severe problems. In order to fix it, she placed me on a twenty-eight day body cleanse and started my treatment. My treatment plan included restoration of all needed fatty acids, vitamins and minerals, and correcting my thyroid functioning. Restoring all of the vitamin/mineral deficiencies and creating proper organ functioning allows the body to naturally replenish the neurotransmitter levels. Once all needed elements were replenished in my body and it was functioning at an optimal level, the plan was to slowly transition off all medications.

In addition to the physiological treatment, my doctor also added a very directive and specific form of meditation. The body has an incredible ability to heal itself. Meditation is one of the key components of helping the body to heal naturally.

CURRENT STATE OF TREATMENT

Medication. Talk therapy.

As heavily utilized as this approach may be, I found **no** success with these methods. Okay, now that we've covered that, let's move on to the success strategies that I have used....

SOLUTION-ORIENTED APPROACHES PHASE ONE

Treatment Team

Develop a "treatment team." This is going to be more than one doctor. Your team members should include a psychiatrist (who embraces integrative medicine) and an integrative medicine doctor. For ways to find these types of doctors, refer to the Index in the back of this book. When you are searching for these doctors, you need to ask them if they are willing to establish open lines of communication with your other doctors. This process may take you a while to find the "like-minded" doctors that you need, but be patient because it is well worth it. It is your life; don't you want to get the most that it has to offer? Your health is *your* responsibility. Your health dictates everything in life. Be aggressive in interviewing your doctors. Remember that you always have a choice. If you do not like one doctor, change! If they don't give you the answers you want, fire them! Cancer patients "shop" for doctors all the time—why shouldn't you?

Let me explain the roles that each member of my team plays.

Psychiatrist

My psychiatrist actually listens for more than fifteen seconds and we have an open dialogue on each facet of my treatment. She is in charge of prescriptions, if they are needed. She is also aware of all of my treatment plans.

Integrative Medicine Doctor

My integrative medicine doctor is in charge of the neurotransmitter, heavy metal toxicity, food allergy, hormone, thyroid and vitamin/mineral testing. She also gives me a lot of time to discuss lifestyle issues such as nutritional intake and exercise and can actually write out a treatment plan that can alleviate all of my deficiencies. I believe that everyone should have an integrative medicine doctor simply to have a healthier, better quality of life. I know that almost everyone in America knows that they should improve their nutritional intake. But most people don't know what to take, how to take it or how much to take to benefit them the most. These doctors can test you and give you an individualized plan to address your specific deficiency issues.

I am over forty, and one of the issues I needed to review was my hormone levels. My integrative medicine doctor also specializes in bioidentical hormone replacement. We are not talking about synthetic hormones such as the ones utilized in HRT (Hormone Replacement Therapy). My doctor realizes that hormones affect mood and thought stability. She does all of my hormone testing and regulates the imbalances.

SOLUTION-ORIENTED
APPROACHES PHASE TWO

The second phase of the treatment solution is to **follow the instructions of your treatment team!** Since you took the time to put this team together, please be smart enough to listen to what they have to say.

Again, I want to restate, you need a team approach in order to have a successful treatment plan. Do exactly what the doctors tell you to do! A lot of people I talk to complain about their lack of success, but when I ask them if they are doing what their doctors instructed them to do they usually say no. Once you have your treatment team in place, how do you expect to be successful if you don't listen to the very people you have selected and entrusted with your health? I trust my treatment team and at this time, I am symptom and episode free!

SOLUTION-ORIENTED
APPROACHES PHASE THREE

The third phase of the solution-oriented approach is to find a mentor or coach who understands what it takes to be successful in dealing with psychological disorders. You need to find someone who has successfully overcome a psychological disorder and understands your special issues. I am not talking about a therapist or a counselor because they generally will not be directive enough and may not have personally experienced or overcome a psychological disorder. This person is not to act as your counselor, psychologist or psychiatrist. What you need to find is a mentor who will help you develop a systematic action plan for your life.

In the business world, people hire mentors because a mentor has reached a level to which their mentee can aspire. Mentoring is important because it can teach you how to reach the objectives regarding what you would like to achieve. This mentoring process may involve career or financial issues on which counselors or therapists cannot ethically advise you. Mentors in the business world have faced all of the challenges, failures and successes that you will be experiencing—and they have emerged victorious. Someone who has been through the trenches can save you a lot of heartache and time and get you to where you want to be.

Now that you have started to successfully manage your illness, you want the rest of your life to reflect that same success; having a mentor is the fastest way to achieve that goal. Most people hire someone like me because they want someone who understands the issues they are facing and can help them put together a success plan that will give them back their life and let them pursue their dreams. For more information on mentoring, go to www.beatbipolartoday.com.

SOLUTION-ORIENTED APPROACHES PHASE FOUR

The next phase of your solution-oriented approach *can* involve support groups. Always use caution when selecting a support group. Many groups become bitch/moan "victim sessions," and never really accomplish anything. Your goal in going to a support group should be to exchange **success strategies** with other individuals who have your illness, not to commiserate about how bad the illness is. This does no one any good.

I am currently serving as the vice president of a DBSA (Depression Bipolar Support Alliance) chapter in a major metropolitan city. I am proud to say our support groups are very proactive and solution-oriented in their approach and our communication with each other. When you leave a support group meeting, you should feel encouraged and uplifted and have new life solutions to try. If you would like to attend a DBSA support group, go to www.dbsalliance.org where they have a listing of all support groups in the United States.

SOLUTION-ORIENTED APPROACH PHASE FIVE

Initially, I started going to an Atlas Orthogonal chiropractor (AOC) for a herniated disc in my back. What I did not realize was the profound effect this type of chiropractic treatment would have on my mood stability. I encourage anyone, not just people who have bipolar disorder, to find an AOC in their area.

The Atlas Orthogonist is a specialist in natural pain relief. The treatment focuses on the first vertebrae in the neck, at the brainstem, through which most of the nerve impulses connecting the brain with the rest of the body travel. The neck has always been a focus area because proper balance and alignment of this area affects so much of the body. The treatments are gentle for patients and are done with a percussion type instrument that releases an energy wave to align the spine, removing nerve pressure. This energy wave places the atlas in an orthogonal (the Greek word for level) position, with the patient feeling no discomfort. The Atlas Orthogonist's methods employ such light touches to the affected area that patients sometimes find it hard to believe that anything effective has been accomplished. Their doubts and fears disappear as quickly as their pain and discomfort.

The Atlas Orthogonist works in a way that speeds and encourages the body's own healing process. The doctor aids that process by gently adjusting the cervical vertebrae back toward normal alignment, thus helping the entire body. Prevention and early detection of misalignments through regular checkups is the key to natural health. Almost anyone can benefit from an Atlas Orthogonal adjustment—not just those who suffer from pain and stiffness in the neck or back, but also those who are afflicted by such common conditions as recurrent headaches, muscular aches of unknown origin, high blood pressure, arthritis, rheumatism and fibromyalgia, just to mention a few.

Again, I have to say, this is one of the greatest discoveries I have ever made!

SOLUTION-ORIENTED APPROACH PHASE SIX

Hyperbaric therapy was another unexpected jewel that I stumbled upon. It took me about six months to finally get in a chamber, but once I did, I was hooked. I could not believe how de-stressed I was, and the feeling of relaxation was unbelievable! I normally have trouble sleeping, but for three straight days, I slept like a baby!

Hyperbaric therapy benefits your body by helping to increase its ability to absorb oxygen. Oxygen is vital for health. It is the single most important element your body needs. Oxygen is our primary source of energy. Not only does oxygen fuel the body, it supports the immune system by destroying toxic substances. Anaerobic bacteria, fungi and viruses all have a common intolerance for oxygen; they cannot survive in an oxygen-rich environment.

The body's vital functions are enhanced by increased availability of oxygen. Increased pressure also stimulates blood flow and decreases inflammation, and has a calming effect. Sleep is enhanced, and absorption of nutrients and digestion is improved. At the cellular level, oxygen is required for proper function. Oxygen deficiency is often overlooked as a root cause of symptoms.

Some of the possible signs of low oxygen levels in the body include:

- premature aging
- unexplainable depression, anger or sadness
- memory loss/forgetfulness
- sleeping disorders, drowsiness, exhaustion
- digestive disorders, acid stomach
- excessive colds or infections
- inflamed, swollen or aching joints
- muscle or tendon aches
- headaches
- chronic fatigue
- difficulty breathing, breathlessness, shortness of breath

Certain environments and activities can contribute to low oxygen levels, including:

- working in a sealed building
- working excessive hours
- high stress work environments
- living in a city with high pollution

- traveling frequently in an airplane

- frequent travel across time zones

- smoking or being around smokers

- consuming alcohol on a regular basis

- driving in congested traffic more than one hour per day

- lack of exercise/sedentary lifestyle

- medical conditions

I know reading this has made you understand how important oxygen is to your body. When I was first asked to try out a chamber, I put the guy off for six months, thinking it wouldn't work. After my first time in the chamber, I understood the miracle of oxygenation of the brain that he was talking about! Run, don't walk, to your nearest hyperbaric therapy center.

Success Summary

- Current diagnostic methods consist of only behavior scales, charts and subjective interpretation.

- On average, it takes eleven years to get an accurate diagnosis of bipolar disorder.

- The following need to be tested: neurotransmitters, thyroid, food allergies, heavy metal toxicity, vitamin and mineral levels and hormones.

- Current state of treatment is medication and talk therapy.

- Solution-oriented approach phase one: develop a treatment team.

- Solution-oriented approach phase two: follow the instructions of the treatment team.

- Solution-oriented approach phase three: find a mentor or coach.

- Solution-oriented approach phase four: find a solution-oriented support group such as a DBSA chapter.

- Solution-oriented approach phase five: source an Atlas Orthogonal chiropractor.

- Solution-oriented approach phase six: spend time in a hyperbaric chamber.

CHAPTER 4
Nutrition

If man made it, don't eat it.

—Jack LaLane

WHAT'S THE PROBLEM?

If you are reading this chapter and are holding in your hand a taco, potato chips, a Twinkie, a candy bar or Cheetos, please put them down and slowly back away. It is time to begin an entirely new approach to your nutritional intake. I am sorry, folks, but the aforementioned items cannot be remotely referred to as nutritional. We have a major problem in this country because most people *do* think that fast food, candy bars, French fries, potato chips, frozen foods, diet sodas, Goldfish, processed food and meats are meeting our nutritional requirements. I got news for you: it ain't happenin'!

By the way, I am sure you have also noticed that if you are taking anti-psychotic medications, your waistline has grown a little (or a lot!) I gained so much weight when I started taking anti-psychotic medication that Pillsbury and Michelin were both calling me to represent their companies! Okay, maybe that's not true, but I did end up of with a face full of fat-ass every time I looked in the mirror. I went from about 14 percent body fat to around 28 percent body fat in six months while maintaining my regular workout schedule. As you might be able to guess, I became a little touchy when somebody mentioned my weight gain.

Somewhere over the years, people in this country got very confused over what foods could be considered nutritional. Do you realize that people in this country are consuming so many preservatives in their food that it now takes a body twice as long to decompose? A nasty thought, but one that should make you think twice before you suck down that next hot dog. Now I ask, nay, I beg of you, to forget every single thing you know about eating. Fasten your seat belt 'cause you're getting ready to take an exciting ride into the world of proper nutrition.

WHAT'S THE BIG DEAL ABOUT NUTRITION?

One of the biggest questions you'll see asked in the print media and the news is *why is proper nutrition necessary?* The problem is that no one ever gets around to answering the question correctly. The purpose of this chapter is to educate you on why proper nutrition is so important to your overall physical *and* mental health.

Building Block of Cells

Food is the building block of all cells in our body. Every cell requires proteins, fats and carbohydrates to reproduce. In layman's terms, you have to consume the proper nutrition in order for your body to work correctly. It is the roadblock between you and illness. In order for your body to work correctly, your neurotransmitters and your hormones have to be working at optimal capacity.

Neurotransmitters

For you to fully understand the importance of this, I'll begin by explaining what neurotransmitters are, what their functions are and why it's important to constantly feed them the energy they need.

Definition

Neurotransmitters are natural chemicals found in the nervous system of the body. Neurotransmitters facilitate and regulate the transfer of electrical energy between the nerve cells (neurons) of the nervous system.

Levels of neurotransmitters that are too low to facilitate the proper transfer of electrical energy between neurons will cause disease and illness. **The only way to truly raise the overall neurotransmitter levels in the brain is to provide the nutrients (amino acids, vitamins and minerals) needed by the body to build neurotransmitters.** Unlike most medications, these nutrients will cross the blood brain barrier into the brain. They are then synthesized into neurotransmitters, which will raise the number of neurotransmitter molecules in the brain. Thus, **providing the proper nutrients for your body accomplishes what prescription drugs are unable to do.**

Now that you know what a neurotransmitter is, here are the five top neurotransmitters that are normally focused on in the medical community.

NEUROTRANS-MITTER	INCORRECT AMOUNTS IN THE BODY CAUSE	PROPER AMOUNTS ARE IN THE BODY CAUSE
Serotonin	• depression • cravings for sweets and carbohydrates • anxiety, irritability, low self–esteem • lack of libido, fatigue • eating disorders • insomnia and obsessive and compulsive actions • suicide, aggression and violence	• Feelings of emotional stability, well-being, personal security, relaxation, calmness, tranquility and confidence
Dopamine	• problems with muscle coordination • depression • mania • hallucinations or extreme behavior of schizophrenia • impulsive, irrational or overly aggressive behavior • tendency to form addictive relationships with pleasurable activities (sex, eating, gambling, etc.) • difficulty sleeping	• libido boost • a sense of satisfaction and increase in assertiveness, short-term memory, concentration and learning • increase in body's growth hormone and ability to repair damaged cells

Noradrenaline	• nervousness • restlessness • difficulty falling asleep • weight loss, depression • lack of energy • reduced libido • sluggish thinking • lack of enthusiasm	• healthy heart rate and blood pressure • glucose conversion to energy • controlled body reactions to stress and anxiety
Glutamine	• cravings for sweets • tendency toward alcoholism • low sex drive	• beneficial effect on mood and energy levels by controlling brain levels of ammonia • increased alertness
Gamma Aminobutyric Acid (GABA)	• sluggish thinking • poor physical coordination • extreme sleepiness • memory problems • panic attacks • exhaustion from stress • excessive stress reactions to normal stress situations	• calmness, reduced anxiety, and relieved nervous tension • better sleep • relaxed muscles

As you can see by reviewing the table, optimal neurotransmitter function is the key to your stable and successful life. Now, what does it take to keep everything balanced and working properly? You guessed it! Proper nutritional intake. During this chapter, I will discuss the role of nutrition and its effects on the body, but only your integrative medicine doctor can develop a treatment plan that best suits your personal biochemistry. Remember, I am not a doctor or a nutritionist; I'm just a guy who has found a successful way to win the battle against bipolar disorder.

WHAT TO EAT

Protein

Amino acids are the building blocks of protein, and it takes protein to allow the body to function properly. Protein stabilizes your blood sugar, revs up your metabolism, slows the absorption of other foods and helps build your muscles.

In order to take all the guesswork out of what you need to eat, here is a list of proteins you can eat.

- beef (organic if possible, and make sure they are lean cuts—we're not talking about a hamburger from McDonald's)

- chicken (organic if possible—breasts are the optimal pieces)

- fish (organic, non farm-raised, if possible—cod, flounder, haddock, halibut, red snapper, salmon, sole, tuna)

- turkey (organic if possible—again, breasts are the optimal pieces)

- egg whites (omelets or boiled eggs without the yolk)

- protein powder (make sure you purchase this at a nutrition store, not your local "superstore." Employees at these stores can help you select the proper protein powders for your body.)

Preparation

If you don't know how to cook, now is the time to learn! In order to be successful with a proper nutrition plan, it is necessary that you cook the majority of your meals. The best way to prepare the foods listed above is to grill, steam, bake or roast them. If you'll notice, frying is not listed as one of your options. I live in the South where most people think the only way you can eat chicken here is to fry it! Don't get me wrong, I eat my share of fried chicken, but that is not how you want to eat it the majority of the time.

I use the following spices and oils to liven up the flavor of this type of cooking:

- sea salt

- cayenne pepper

- olive oil (gives chicken and steak a wonderful flavor)

- Balsamic vinegar

- organic Italian dressing (great marinade for steak and chicken)

- *real* butter (organic)

I personally buy all of my meats, dressings, spices and oils from an organic grocery. This ensures that I am not consuming any unwanted toxins or synthetic hormones. There are plenty of organic cookbooks available to help you with preparation and variation.

Carbohydrates

Over the last several years, carbohydrates have taken a bad rap in the media. The rage in the U.S. has been "low carbohydrate or no carbohydrate" diets. Carbohydrates have been blamed for the weight-gain epidemic that has rolled across the United States. Now, forget all of the bad things you have heard about carbohydrates, and I'll show you the truth about why they are so important for your body's proper functioning.

Your brain cannot function without carbohydrates. The brain needs a certain amount of glucose (sugar), found in your blood, to function properly. If your body does not receive the amount of carbohydrates it needs, it will start to break down protein—and the easiest protein to break down is muscle. Muscle is the metabolic furnace that's going to help you lose fat. Therefore, if you're not eating the right kind of carbohydrates in the correct amounts, you are sabotaging your own physical and mental health as well as destroying your own fat-burning machine!

Carbohydrates normally fit into two categories: simple and complex. Simple carbohydrates are the ones to avoid. The following is a list of simple carbohydrates:

- white sugar
- white bread
- crackers
- cookies
- products made from refined flour and sugar such as bakery products (cakes, donuts)
- candy
- processed cereal
- ice cream
- white rice
- white pasta

This list is not all-inclusive, but these are the main carbohydrates people tend to consume. These foods also have a tendency to be loaded with preservatives. If you've ever noticed, about thirty minutes after you eat this type of carbohydrate, your energy level and mood tend to decrease. Simple carbohydrates release into your bloodstream very quickly and cause your insulin levels to spike. In simple terms (no pun intended), too much insulin causes damage to your body, as well as fat storage and weight gain.

Complex carbohydrates, on the other hand, help you sustain energy over several hours. Here are some of the complex carbohydrates you need to incorporate into your eating plan:

- oatmeal (Raw oats—nothing processed. I sprinkle organic brown sugar on mine to flavor it and use real butter. Oatmeal is the greatest carbohydrate I have ever found!)

- brown and wild rice

- new potatoes (with skin)

- sweet potatoes, yams

- beans (all types)

- peas (all types)

- lentils

- whole grain pasta (best if purchased from organic food store)

- whole grain bread (must contain all organic ingredients)

- green vegetables (eat as many as you like!)

With simple carbohydrates, you notice that your energy level plummets after you eat them. With complex carbohydrates, this does not happen. Complex carbohydrates release into the bloodstream very slowly, keeping insulin levels even and giving the body a stable source of energy. **When insulin levels remain stable, increased mood stability will follow.** Complex carbohydrates not only provide you with energy throughout the day, but they also help you burn fat!

Preparation

The best way to prepare complex carbohydrates is to steam or bake. I suggest purchasing a steamer for convenience. You can place your food in the steamer, set the timer and move on to another task! They are the best invention in the kitchen; I use mine almost every single day. You may want to use some of the same spices, dressings or oils I listed in the Protein section to flavor your food.

Fats

Just like carbohydrates, fats have taken a beating in the media. Your body *must* have the proper amount of fats to be able to function. There are good fats (more commonly known as essential fatty acids) and bad fats. You want to avoid the bad fats and make sure you get several servings of the good fats in your eating plan every day. Your brain is composed of about 60 percent fat so, in order for your brain to function at its optimal level, you must ingest the proper amount of fats each day. **The body cannot manufacture fats** and this is why it is so important to take in the good fats every day.

Let's start with the "bad guys." The bad fats:

- partially saturated fats

- saturated fats

- trans-fatty acids

You find these bad fats in fried foods, pork, processed cheese, cream and processed butter, luncheon meats, margarine, French fries, mayonnaise, potato chips and some salad dressings. This would include most foods at fast-food restaurants. These types of fats should be avoided at all costs!

Now for the "good guys." The good fats:

- polyunsaturated fats

- monounsaturated fats

- flax seeds or flax seed oil (make sure it is cold pressed)

- fish oils (These should be purchased at a health food or organic store. I take mine in capsule form.)

- avocadoes

- olive oil (I do most of my cooking with olive oil)

- olives

- walnuts, almonds, cashews and other nuts and seeds (make sure they are raw and not sugar coated or salted)

- salmon, mackerel and sardines

I will say it again: **your body must have essential fatty acids on a daily basis in order to function at its peak levels.** I normally get my daily allowance of these fats through capsule form, by adding flax seed oil to my protein shakes or by ingesting nuts, olives or fish.

Vegetables and Salads

Vegetables will always have a special place in my memory. I don't know if you guys were ever told this, but I heard, "If you don't eat your vegetables, you're going to get a whoopin'," almost every day of my childhood—and that was the motivating factor for me eating those green things on my plate. To this day, I don't think my parents understood why it was so important for me to eat my vegetables. I think it was just passed down from generation to generation. Just in case you haven't figured out why we need to eat our vegetables, here's the reason.

You can eat all the vegetables you want; they have very few "usable" calories so they do not count towards your caloric intake during the day. I take advantage of this by steaming broccoli, covering it with real butter and eating it whenever I want! Vegetables slow down the digestive process, which is great for the fat-burning process. The fiber in the vegetables keeps your blood sugar stable and your insulin under control, **thus helping with mood stability.** Because vegetables are so fibrous, they scrub your intestines clean as they work their way through your body. You can absorb more vitamins and nutrients if your intestines are clean. So, go pick up the phone, call your mamma, and say "Thank you for making me eat my vegetables when I was a kid!"

Veggies for you to eat:

- lettuce and leafy greens (not iceberg lettuce)
- green beans
- carrots
- spinach
- asparagus

- broccoli

- cauliflower

- cabbage

- peppers

- zucchini

- mushrooms

- squash

- onions

- tomatoes

- edamame (soybeans)

Preparation

Fresh, organic vegetables are always the best way to go, but if you don't have access to them, go with frozen veggies instead of canned. Canned vegetables tend to be heavily salted and contain preservatives.

The best way to prepare vegetables is by steaming them. You can use the steamer you already bought to cook your complex carbohydrates! Steaming helps preserve the nutritional ingredients in the vegetables.

Fruits

There are lots of natural sugars in fruits, but they're high in fiber and they taste good! Your daily eating plan should always contain fruit. They also make a great dessert! An organic apple a day can really help to keep the doctor away! (Here's another "shout out" to your mamma for knowing what is best for you!)

Here are the fruits that my integrative medicine doctor suggests that I eat:

- cherries

- oranges

- grapefruit (some studies have shown that eating grapefruit promotes fat loss)

- peaches

- apples

- tangerines

- apricots

- bananas

- strawberries

- blueberries

- blackberries

Preparation

Always wash the fruit thoroughly and only purchase organic fruit. I consume all of my fruits raw.

Vitamins and Minerals

Due to the complexity of each person's individual biochemistry, in this section, I will only be listing the vitamins and minerals and how they work in the body. **You should consult with your integrative medicine doctor about the intake of the proper levels and amounts of each specific vitamin and mineral for your particular situation** because it is different for every person. Your integrative medicine doctor is the correct person to conduct the proper testing of vitamin and mineral levels. In order to utilize this process successfully, you must be under the care of a medical doctor.

VITAMIN/ MINERAL	INCORRECT AMOUNTS IN THE BODY LINKED TO	CORRECT AMOUNTS IN THE BODY ASSIST IN
Vitamin A and Mixed Carotenoids		• healthy vision • cell reproductions • immune function • wound healing • protecting body from stress damage from free radicals, toxic chemicals and immune dysfunction • metabolism of essential fatty acids
Vitamin B Complex	• symptoms of mild depression • irritability • apathy • anxiety • fatigue • other symptoms related to mood depression	• creating more mood-elevating effects than most other nutrients • promoting proper nerve function and nerve cell metabolism, which produces optimal neurotransmitter levels
Thiamine (B1)	• impaired mental function possibly leading to psychosis	• enabling brain cells to produce energy

Riboflavin (B2)		• metabolizing essential fatty acids • promoting antioxidant (ability to neutralize free radicals) properties of glutathione
Niacin (B3)	• symptoms of psychosis dementia, and specific forms of schizophrenia (long-term deficiencies)	• regulating blood sugar levels and energy production • indirectly affecting serotonin levels
Pantothenic Acid (B5)		• along with niacin, forming coenzymes necessary for proper functioning of essential fatty acids, metabolism of carbohydrates and production of adrenal hormones • managing extreme stress
Pyridoxine	• depression (deficiency)	• correcting brain metabolism dysfunctions that can cause depression • heightening serotonin function by slowing destruction of tryptophan in the brain • helping enzymes that convert tryptophan to serotonin as well as tyrosine to noradrenaline

Cobalamin or cyanocobalamin (B12)	• neurological problems, confusion, depression and memory loss (deficiency) • Alzheimer's' disease in elderly (deficiency)	• metabolizing of essential fatty acids and folic acid, which has important effects on mood • creation of myelin sheath that insulates nerve fibers and allows for the free flow of neurotransmitters • treating fatigue, depression and infertility • possibly helping body secrete additional melatonin
Folic Acid or Folate	• lowered brain levels of serotonin and S-adenosyl-methionine (SAM), the amino acid metabolite with mood-elevating properties (deficiency) • major depression (surplus) • psychiatric symptoms among nonpsychiatric patients (deficiency)	• regulation of functions relating to mood • along with B12, stimulating formation of a compound necessary for the first step in synthesizing neurotransmitters, especially serotonin • alleviating symptoms of depression • possibly preventing Alzheimer's disease
Choline	• memory loss or mood disorders • depression and lack of concentration	• controlling mood swings • improving overall disposition • boosting moods of Alzheimer's patients

NADH/Coen-zyme 1		• boosting memory and elevating mood • slowing aging as a potent antioxidant • cell production of energy • creating antidepressant effects through its action on the brain and central nervous system • body production of important mood-boosting brain chemicals • improving motor skills, thinking, memory and mood in Parkinson's and Alzheimer's patients • reducing symptoms of depression
Vitamin C	• depressed mood	• synthesizing the neurotransmitters Noradrenaline and Dopamine • metabolizing of essential fatty acids • strengthening adrenal and other endocrine glands • mood elevation
Vitamin D	• mild depression • loss of appetite and interest in sex • insomnia associated with Seasonal Affective Disorder	• (Sunlight reacts with skin cells to produce Vitamin D.)

Vitamin E	• limited serotonin activity (deficiency)	• virtually all tissue functions in body • boosting immunity, reducing heart disease and possibly enhancing athletic performance • main protection of brain cell membranes • possibly slowing Alzheimer's disease
Coenzyme Q10 (CoQ10)	• fatigue, mental lethargy and depression (deficiency)	• playing a major role in overall metabolism, heart health and immune function • helping the body's cells use oxygen and generate energy • acting as a catalyst for body process which produce ATP, necessary for energy at cellular level
Calcium	• aggravated rather than balanced mood in a person with too much noradrenaline activity (large doses)	• a smoothly functioning nervous system, sufficient serotonin activity and prevention of irritability and depression • slight sedation if taken before bed

Magnesium	• anxiety, irritability, fatigue and depression (deficiency)	• blood sugar balance, production of omega-3 essential fatty acid DHA and nervous system function • possibly improving premenstrual symptoms related to mood changes
Iron	• anemia • fatigue • lethargy and other symptoms shared by depression • impaired learning ability, attention span and mental development	• supplying cells with oxygen and producing energy (major role) • producing neurotransmitters (indirect role)
Selenium	• increased symptoms of anxiety and depression	• protecting against age-related ailments such as heart disease, cancer and arthritis
Chromium	• blood sugar swings, obesity and diabetes • (Mental stress and large amounts of sugary foods deplete body's chromium stores.)	• proper insulin function • reducing blood pressure-increasing effects of high sugar intake • controlling hunger, reducing body fat and encouraging muscle development

Water

Water is essential in every metabolic function in your body. The body is over 70 percent water, and most people don't even come close to taking in the sufficient amount of water on a daily basis. Sodas, juice, teas, sports drinks, flavored waters, beer, wine and milk *do not* qualify as replacements for water. The average person needs to take in a minimum of ten, eight-ounce cups of pure water every day. When you first wake up in the morning, drink eight ounces of distilled water immediately. Your body gets dehydrated during sleep and needs the rehydration. The only way your body can expel fat is through sweat or urination. It is impossible to expel fat without consuming enough water throughout the day! Proper water consumption also allows the body to keep an elevated metabolic rate, enabling your body to become a fat-burning machine.

I drink three different types of water—distilled, oxygenated and spring water that I purchase from my local grocery store or organic grocery. **Do not drink tap water!** Tap water is loaded with contaminants, toxins, poisons and chlorine. In addition, you may want to consider purchasing a water purification system to use in your home.

HOW AND WHEN TO EAT

I eat five small meals a day. This allows my body to continually receive and burn fuel. It also helps speed up my metabolism, allowing me to maintain or lose weight, and gives my body the fuel it needs to function properly. Because I'm feeding my body throughout the day and controlling my insulin levels, I have more control over my mood stability.

I follow two simple rules when eating. Rule one: I consume only organic food when possible. Rule two: I divide my plate into thirds: one-third protein, one-third complex carbohydrates and one-third vegetable, salad or fruit. I generally eat about every two or three hours.

I live a very busy life, so I have to plan ahead and sometimes prepare foods to take with me to eat during the day. When I say "meal,"

I do not necessarily mean that you have to sit down for hours to eat. I keep a travel cooler with me at all times, filled with my pre-planned meals. That way, I'm not stuck somewhere with nothing but bad choices surrounding me, tempting me to eat things that will negatively affect my mood.

Here is a "daily sample" of what I eat:

- Breakfast (6 A.M.)**

  Oatmeal with butter and brown sugar and an egg-white omelet that contains fresh vegetables and real butter, OR a Labrada Nutrition Lean Body MRP shake (meal replacement) that I mix with bananas and one cup of dry oatmeal (see Index for information on Labrada products).

  *MVM aloe capsules (2) (see Index or **www. beatbipolartoday.com** for information) and supplements as directed by my integrative medicine doctor.

  *One ounce LiquiVida aloe juice (see Index or **www. beatbipolartoday.com** for information)

- Mid-morning meal (9:00 A.M. - 10:00 A.M.)**

  Protein shake, organic apple and a handful of almonds

- Lunch (12:00 P.M. - 1:00 P.M.)**

  Six-ounce portion of beef, chicken, turkey or fish, baked sweet potato with real butter, green salad or vegetable

- Mid-afternoon meal (3:00 P.M. - 4:00 P.M.)**

  Six-ounce portion of beef, chicken or turkey, fruit, and a handful of nuts, OR a Labrada Lean Body MRP Shake

- Dinner (6:00 P.M. - 7:00 P.M.)

  Six-ounce portion of beef, chicken, fish or turkey (I like to eat turkey at night because it contains tryptophan which promotes relaxation), green vegetable and green salad

- Before Bedtime (9:00 P.M. - 10:00 P.M.)

  If I am still hungry, I'll drink a small protein shake (not a meal replacement shake) and take all directed supplements. I use Pro V60 by Labrada Nutrition, which is a nighttime formula that promotes muscle strengthening without aspartame.

  *One-ounce LiquiVida aloe juice and MVM aloe capsules (2).

* I use aloe products from Liquidity International. The LiquiVida aloe juice and the MVM aloe capsules aid in the delivery of oxygen to your body's blood cells which then deliver oxygen to all other cells of the body. It is impossible for the body's cells to be healthy without a proper supply of oxygen. Oxygen is crucial in helping the body resist diseases.

**Sometimes when my energy seems low during the day, I will drink an energy drink. There is only one drink on the market that I will consume and it is made by Quixtar. It contains no sugar or additives and consists primarily of B vitamins. You can find more information on this drink in the Index.

HELPFUL TIPS

I cook most of my meals on Sunday for the upcoming week. This takes the stress out of trying to juggle my schedule and prepare meals every night. I usually have more time on Sundays than any other day of the week, so it is natural for me to utilize that time to prevent in advance the stress that I would feel during the week trying to manage meal preparation. Sometimes, I even get my organic grocery store to steam or prepare foods for me—and they do it at no charge!

I like to work with my clients in helping them to find strategies to prevent stressors from happening before they ever occur. Healthy eating should not be a source of stress, but a source of energy that allows you to feel great, stabilize your mood, and have an abundance of energy. When you eat properly, visualize every single bite of food you chew as fuel for your dreams, moving you closer to regaining control of your life!

Success Summary

- Nutritional intake is the most important weapon against bipolar disorder.

- Food is the building block of all cells in our body.

- Neurotransmitters depend on proper nutritional intake to reproduce and function properly.

- Proteins are the building blocks of your muscles.

- Carbohydrates provide fuel for the body.

- EFAs (essential fatty acids) are vital for proper brain and body function.

- Vegetables are free calories and can be consumed any time.

- Fruits are high in fiber and taste great!

- Vitamin and mineral needs must be addressed in order for the body to function at optimal levels.

- Your body is over 70 percent water and you need to consume at least ten to eight ounce glasses of pure water per day.

- Eat five to six small meals per day.

- Preparation is the key to achieving your nutritional intake goals!

CHAPTER 5
Exercise

> One does what one is; one becomes what one does.
>
> —Robert von Musil

WHAT DOES "GOOD FOR YOU" MEAN TO ME?

Just like nutrition, the word exercise appears repeatedly in the news media, infomercials and books, and is talked about by almost everyone you know. It is one of the most talked about, least-acted upon subjects I've ever seen. Fitness centers and gyms are always packed to the rim in January, February, and March. By April, most people have long forgotten their New Year's resolutions to get back into shape and lead a healthy lifestyle. So why is exercise so expendable in most peoples' lives? It's because people really just do not understand the overall picture of how exercise affects the body and mind. If people really understood this fact, you couldn't keep them out of the gyms or keep them from exercising outside every day!

Recent research by Harvard University indicates that exercise is the biological equivalent of antidepressant medications.

To help you along this process, I am going to explain why exercise is so important to the human body. Everyone always hears about nutrition and exercise, but no one ever tells us what to do, how to do it or why do it. So let's start with the whys of exercise. They're called endorphins....

Endorphins

Endorphins are peptides (amino acid compounds) that are known to relieve pain but also affect mood and the body's response to stress. There are twenty types of endorphins, beta-endorphin being the most mood-elevating. Endorphins are short-lived in the body and need to be reproduced. They play a primary role in the following:

- aging
- circulation of blood
- cravings due to stress or starvation
- immunity
- pregnancy and labor
- reproductive hormone cycles
- timing of appetite

Here's how to increase the production of endorphins:

- nutritional supplements
- overall physical, mental and emotional wellbeing
- laughter
- sex (should I list this as number #1?)

- exercise

- pain (once you experience pain, endorphins help relieve pain)

So, if endorphins are key components of mood stability, and exercise is a chief way to increase endorphin levels, why wouldn't you exercise every day?

The endorphin killer? Stress. So, since I assume most all of you have stress in your life, there is just another reason why you should exercise!

Here is another reason why you should exercise: studies have found that low levels of endorphins correlate with depression, anxiety, phobias and obsessive-compulsive behaviors. On the other hand, studies have shown that exercise correlates with improved mood, decreased anxiety, improved sleep, improved resiliency in the face of stress and increased self-esteem. Do you still need convincing? If you laugh and have sex while you are exercising, just think how healthy you will be while you're producing three times the amounts of endorphins you normally would! I haven't tried this myself yet, but I am definitely thinking about giving it a shot!

More benefits of exercise...

- strengthens your heart and lungs

- burns body fat (just thirty minutes a day can give you a stronger, leaner you, which will also help elevate your mood!)

- builds muscle (remember, that's what helps to burn fat!)

- switches your body from fat-storing to fat-burning mode

- increases positive self-esteem

- relieves stress and improves mood

- helps stimulate one of the two fat-removing processes of your body—sweating! (The other is urinating. That's why you need to drink water all day!)

- increases relaxation

- reduces anxiety

- improves quality of life

Are you starting to understand why exercise is so critical? Just in case I still haven't sold you on why exercise is so important, here is another little tidbit: over three hundred thousand deaths per year are directly related to obesity. That figure doesn't include heart attacks, diabetes, and other illnesses brought on by obesity.

SO WHAT'S HOLDING YOU BACK?

Now I've given you all of the reasons why you should exercise. Let's discuss what's been holding you back and address all of the excuses/reasons/habits and negative self-talk. Once we've addressed these, they will no longer hold you back and you will be able to achieve the fitness level you desire.

Lack of Correct Information

If you're waiting to get accurate exercise information from most magazines, TV and infomercials, you are looking in the wrong place! I know many people who had a friend who had a cousin who had a nephew who was a trainer, and he provided you with all of the wrong information about exercise and how to work out. So how do we fix this? Most bodybuilding magazines are very good sources for information regarding exercise and weight loss. I have my own personal trainer who is a certified nutritionist and who is listed among the top fifty-five trainers in the world. I feel very fortunate to have found him, and he is one of my best friends. His contact information will be listed in the Index in case you have any questions about exercise, sourcing trainers or nutrition.

So how do you find a *qualified* personal trainer? My personal preference for finding trainers is to locate a gym that caters to top athletes and bodybuilders. This may be a little intimidating at first, but it can pay huge dividends if you can find a trainer that you gel with and who helps you to achieve your goals. Many trainers can work wonders in twelve weeks **if you do what they tell you to do.** You must be committed and willing to follow their instructions. Just like your treatment team, be smart enough to do what they tell you. The training, in combination with your balanced vitamin/mineral/hormone levels and proper nutrition, will go a long way in helping you to reach your goals that much quicker.

Inability to Get Motivated and Stay Motivated

Remember back in Chapter 1 where you had to decide what you really wanted? This also applies to fitness. You have to totally commit to achieving your goals and improving your quality of life—no matter what it takes! Until you are ready to do this, stay on the couch, eat your Twinkies and don't waste anyone else's time.

Now, if you have decided to get up off the couch, use one of the strategies that I suggest to my clients. Develop a "Vision Board." I have a Vision Board myself that I look at every day; it helps me to visualize where I want my life to be.

One of my heroes when I first became interested in bodybuilding was a professional bodybuilder named Lee Labrada. I was a "wanna-be" bodybuilder, and to me, Lee had the greatest body I'd ever seen. I knew that Lee Labrada was a very motivated individual. He credited his desire to excel to his humble beginnings. He came to the United States with his family at the age of two, after fleeing the Communist regime in his native Cuba. The family, stripped of all of its possessions, settled in Chicago and had to completely rebuild their lives. Following his father's example, Labrada learned that through hard work and a strong vision, a person can achieve any dream imaginable. Today, Labrada continues this life philosophy and strives to pass it on to others.

Not only did I admire his body, but I admired his mind, his work ethic, his determination and his spirit. I read everything that I could about him and what made him successful. This was the type of guy I wanted to be and have as one of the mentors surrounding me. (For more information regarding Lee's story and his company, go to www. labrada.com.)

Now, I'm twenty years older and I have a picture of Lee (at twenty years older also!) on my Vision Board...and he still looks phenomenal! So, my picture of Lee on my Vision Board represents to me a visual picture of what I want my body to look like and the health-conscious lifestyle I want to emulate. When I don't feel like going to the gym, I can see in my mind Lee's body and imagine his determination and lifestyle, and that helps to motivate me to keep going. It is a very important part of the "what do you really want?" question we discussed in the first chapter.

So here's how to make a Vision Board. Sit down, get quiet and begin to dream about how you want your life to be—no matter how ridiculous, impossible or unattainable it seems to be, figure out what it is and begin to collect visual representations of those things or goals. If you want to get married, cut out pictures of brides and grooms. If you want a body like a Victoria's Secret model, cut out pictures of them. If you want a gym in your own home, cut out pictures of the equipment and how you want it laid out. You're probably beginning to get the concept. Don't forget, this can apply to every area of your life—not just your fitness goals. Paste these pictures on some poster board and put them where you will see them every day. You'll be surprised after you visualize and feel the emotions every day how much faster you will meet your fitness and other life goals. But always remember, as I said in an earlier chapter, that you must fuel these visualizations with emotion! So, load up your iPod with blood-pumping music, get your dream in your mind's eye and head to the gym!

Fear

> *Action conquers fear.*
>
> —Peter N. Zarlenga

I talk to so many people who let fear stop them from ever trying a different course in life. I normally hear the following (and I have listed some of my normal responses):

- I failed before, so why should I try again?

- It's the meds; there's nothing I can do.

- I will never be able to continue, so why bother even starting?

- What if people make fun of me?

- People in the gym just aren't very friendly. (You're not there to make friends.)

- I'm just too depressed. (If your house is burning down, would you be too depressed to get out of it in time? If the answer is no, get your butt up and go exercise.)

- I don't have the money. (Last time I looked, walking was free!)

Action is the chief way to overcome fear. *Action makes you focus on the goal, not the problem.* At some point, you have to decide: do I want to live in this "comfortable hell" or do I want to step out and take the needed action to achieve my goal, which will lead me to a better life? I cannot make this decision for you, nor can I talk you into it. You and only you can finally sum up the courage to say, "That's it...I've had enough. I am not going to live this way any more. I am going to change and I'm going to do it starting today. Right now." It's up to you.

> *He that is good for making excuses is seldom good for anything else.*
>
> —Benjamin Franklin

Excuses come in the form of "I don't have time to exercise. I don't feel good. I'm just too fat. It's just too hard. I've tried everything and nothing works…" and on and on. My suggestion for this is to manage it like you deal with your fears. Always remember that non-achievers use situations to quit and achievers use their situations as a reason to win. Don't think that I haven't been there myself—remember, I lost everything. I had every good excuse in the world to quit, go on disability and give up. I thank God every day that I didn't. Now, I have a greater life than I ever imagined and it continues to get better every day.

EXERCISE—HOW TO GET STARTED

There are two types of exercise—aerobic and anaerobic. Aerobic exercise includes activities like walking, running, swimming and cycling. Anaerobic exercise includes activities like weight lifting or any activity that provides resistance for your muscles. In order to lose weight, build muscle and increase overall fitness levels, you must incorporate both aerobic and anaerobic activity in your exercise plan. For those who have had a long layoff from activity, I always suggest starting your exercise plan with a walk every day. Always remember, you didn't get in the shape you are in right now overnight, so do not get discouraged if miracles don't happen overnight. Now, I didn't say a stroll, I said a walk…you need to be walking fast enough to increase your heart and breathing rates. Most people start out walking twenty minutes a day and some even increase their time to an hour a day. This all comes down to personal preference.

Winners are those people who make a habit of doing the things losers are uncomfortable doing.

—Ed Foreman

Your Action Plan

The simplest plan for most people to follow is the one I use personally.

- Day 1

    Ten minutes of cardio warm-up (this means walking on a treadmill, riding an indoor bicycle, etc.) and then thirty to forty-five minutes of weight training. I work each muscle group once a week (this is where your personal trainer comes in).

- Day 2

    Same as Day 1

- Day 3

    Cardio only—I do at least thirty minutes.

- Day 4

    Same as Day 1

- Day 5

    Same as Day 1

- Day 6

    Thirty minutes of cardio

- Day 7

    Rest.

This is the plan that I follow. Some plans contain only three days of weight training paired with three days of cardio training. Your personal workout plan will depend on what you want to accomplish and how much time you have to devote to your goals.

My personal trainer offers exercise manuals that are available through my website (www.beatbipolartoday.com) that can lead you through a workout for each muscle group if you need additional guidance. Please consult your personal trainer for his suggestions or consult my trainer's web site at www.evolve-now.com.

As always, consult your doctor before beginning any exercise program.

Success Summary

- Exercise needs to be a staple of a "mind-body-soul" approach.

- Exercise produces endorphins.

- Exercise relieves stress, improves mood, reduces anxiety, increases self-esteem, burns fat and improves quality of life.

- A personal trainer can help you achieve your fitness goals at a much faster pace.

- Create a "Vision Board" to help you stay motivated on the tough days.

- Action makes you focus on the goal, not the problem!

- Excuses aren't reasons, they're just excuses!

- You must incorporate aerobic and anaerobic activity in your exercise plan.

- Consult your doctor before beginning any exercise program.

CHAPTER 6
Faith

MY STORY

It was July 15th, 1986, and I can still remember sitting in that small, brick Southern Baptist church in Greensboro, North Carolina, listening to the preacher talk about how a relationship with Christ could bring peace, joy, love and meaning to a person's life. I had entered the church that morning a defeated man who had just lost his girlfriend, thought a gin bottle could bring happiness, had a father who was dying, had lost any reason to live, was actively contemplating suicide and was wondering why anyone would want to endure life any longer than they had to.

As the preacher spoke, my thoughts went back to how I had ended up attending the service that day. A guy I worked with had been trying for about a year to get me to go to church with him, but I kept refusing. My life was all about "sex, drugs and rock-n-roll," and at the time that seemed pretty fun. I basically told him to take Jesus and stick Him up his ass. I told him that the church was nothing but a bunch of Bible-thumping hypocrites. I was actually more attracted to the church of Satan than I was the church of Christ. It seemed to suit me better at that point in my life.

On top of all of that, I hated most Christians. Over the course of my life, very few Christians had ever shown me any love or kindness; I had a big chip on my shoulder towards these hypocritical jerks. As you can guess, my attitudes didn't stop him from asking me to go to his church with him every week. So for one solid year, he just stayed on my case about it until one day I finally said, "Okay, I'll go if it will get you off my back."

So there I was, sitting there hearing a message of hope for the future. The preacher described a future full of promise, a church and people who would love and care about me, a God who loved me regardless of what I had done in the past and a Savior who died for me. You have to understand that when I was growing up, very few people had ever showed any love to me, so everything he was saying touched something deep down inside of me in an area of my heart that I didn't know existed. I could feel the tears streaming down my face and this queasy, nervous churning in my stomach as he started to give the invitation. Before I knew it, I had jumped out of the pew and was running down the aisle toward the preacher. He grabbed my hand, pulled me close and asked me if I wanted to ask Jesus into my heart. I shook my head yes and he proceeded to lead me in a prayer that would ask Jesus to come into my heart and would change my life forever. I have a copy of a prayer similar to the one I prayed that morning listed in the Index of this book.

I AM NOT POLITICALLY CORRECT

I am fully aware that not everyone reading this book is a Christian. That being said, I *am* a Christian, and I want to address the role that Christ can play in your life—and more specifically, the role He can play in the management of your illness. I have only one answer whenever anyone has asked me any of these questions:

- How did you keep from killing yourself in the midst of your deepest depression?

- How did you stop doing drugs and being an alcoholic?

- How did you find purpose in your life?

- How did you keep from having an episode or killing yourself after you lost several hundred thousand dollars?

- How did you find the strength to go on living every day with your illness?

- How do you find hope after you were diagnosed?

My answer has always been, and will always be, Jesus Christ.

I'M PISSED OFF AT GOD

God doesn't play dice.

—Albert Einstein

Most of the people I encounter in the mental illness community have mixed emotions about God. Many feel that He has abandoned them and cursed them with an awful illness. I, too, felt that way when I first received my diagnosis. I walked around asking, "Why me?" I think I spent at least two years walking around, moaning and groaning, whining and complaining about "what God had done to me." I was riding on the "life is unfair" train and it stopped at the stations of Self-Pity, Commiseration, Disappointment, Resentment and Anger quite frequently. Being a victim was becoming easier and easier each day. It absolved me of personal responsibility for my life and my illness. Are you as disgusted with my behavior as I came to be?

I hope so, because I found an interesting scripture while I was reading my Bible one day that helped me come to grips with having bipolar disorder.

> *I'm your Creator, you were in my care*
> *even before you were born.*
>
> —Isaiah 44:2 NIV

All of a sudden, I realized that long before my parents had conceived me, I was conceived in the mind of God. I realized that I was not an accident or a mistake and that my bipolar disorder was no surprise to God. God makes each of us for greatness, and He had a plan for my life that involved my illness. I did not realize that it would take ten years for Him to reveal how I could use my illness to inspire others. But He did. He knew the plan all along.

I soon changed my thoughts to the attitude of "why not me". I could have been diagnosed with something far worse than bipolar disorder. I thought about the all the children I taught who had multiple physical and mental handicaps, and what they faced on a daily basis. These children could not walk, talk, feed themselves or manage their own personal hygiene. Being in that type of environment can end any sense of pity you feel for yourself very quickly. And out of all of the children who had these difficulties, I had never heard them complain. Not once.

I once taught a little girl named Ryan. Her only method of communication with the outside world was blinking her eyes and smiling. When I would enter the room, she would begin blinking furiously and smiling, and I knew she was happy to see me. I have never forgotten her. A few years later, when I received my diagnosis and was working through the "why me" phase, I kept thinking about Ryan and her struggles and how much happiness she brought to my life. How, then, could I complain about my diagnosis? I felt like slapping myself for my ingratitude for the things that I *had* been given.

Once you begin to grasp the concept of gratitude, it is your key to freedom from the chains of who you are now and unlocks who you can be.

PURPOSE

So many people get up each day without any direction or clue about what is going to transpire. They go from day to day to day, enduring life, never stopping to grasp the purpose of life and what it has to offer. Most peoples' lives are filled with hopelessness, emptiness and fear. How wonderful it would be if people would finally wake up and realize that there is a purpose for life, and that God wants you to find that purpose and have a great life? Now if you get up with that thought in mind every morning, life is not just endured any more: it is truly enjoyed.

Your purpose normally involves something that you are already very passionate about, and it's usually an activity or vocation that you would perform even if you were not being paid to do it. God will use your talents that you already have and enjoy using. God will not lead you to become something without aiding you to become the "best" you can possibly be in that area. He will not give you a talent and then fail to give you opportunities for discovering, using, developing, practicing and perfecting it.

When people ask me how they find their purpose in life, I tell them that first, they have to have a relationship with Jesus Christ. Then just ask God to show you your purpose. If you ask, God will reveal this to you…but you need to be ready for the answer.

This is not something to be taken lightly. I was hoping that God was going to tell me that my purpose was to be an investment banker and spend most of my time on the beach in Hawaii! I did not realize that finding my purpose would include me ministering to gang members; working with autistic children; feeding, bathing and changing the diapers of handicapped children; and spending countless hours working with emotionally disturbed students. This was a long way from me sticking my toes in the sand outside my beach house while making loads of cash! But even though it wasn't what *I* envisioned, God's plans are always perfect; I don't think I could have been any happier doing anything else. When you are doing God's will, you have a peace inside of you that really does go beyond any understanding.

I asked God to show me my special purpose. Before I knew it, I was volunteering at a school for severely handicapped children. This led to me pursue my degree in special education, which led me to being asked to be an assistant basketball coach with one of the top women's basketball programs in the state. This change then led me to a head-coaching position during which I went to the state championship game, which led me to a career change in another state, which led me to another successful coaching career, which led me to being prepared to teach, mentor and inspire others about psychological disorders and their management. All of these events led me to writing this book. Are you starting to see how all of these things string together and build upon each other? God used my already innate talents of speaking and motivating people to teach, coach and mentor all types of people. And through all of these changes, He knew the entire plan.

I love the analogy that finding your purpose is like driving a car from New York to California at night. When you're driving that car, the headlights only shine about two hundred feet in front of the car. So you can literally drive from one side of the country to the other by only seeing about two hundred feet in front of you. God works on a "need to know" basis, and He will give you the two hundred feet of information while you're driving!

More than likely, you are not going to have a "Charlton Heston moment" when God speaks to you in a booming, theatrical voice telling you your "ultimate purpose" in life. He is probably going to quietly lead you from opportunity, to person, to book, to pastor, to child, to a career, all of which will ultimately take you to where you need to be.

Whenever I have to make a decision that involves my life's purpose, I feel a mental, physical and spiritual ease or unease, and I pay attention to that. Some people use meditation or prayer to improve this ability to listen to God. After I have done my initial prayer and meditation, I sometimes discuss my feelings with my closest friends or pastor.

ANGER

> *Everyone should be quick to listen, slow to speak and slow to become angry.*
>
> —James 1:19 NIV

Anger seems to be one of the first emotions that people initially experience when they are diagnosed. The anger that you feel can be coming from many different sources. You could be mad at your doctor because he is wrong about the diagnosis (denial), mad at your friends or family for taking you to the hospital or for making you see a doctor against your will, or mad at God because He made you—and why in the world would He ever give you an illness like this? You could be mad about the way you think you are going to be treated or perceived by your friends, family and the public.

Maybe you have accepted your diagnosis, but you're angry, just like I was, because you feel like the doctors are not listening when you describe the side effects that the medicine is causing. Perhaps you feel that "normal" human emotions that you experience, such as sadness, frustration and even jubilation, are always attributed to "depression and mania" instead of healthy, regular feelings that all humans experience; and this causes resentment and anger in you.

Anger is one of the "frequency feelings" I wrote about earlier in this book. It is one of the negative emotions that acts as a sign from the Universe to us that we are on the wrong track emotionally and cognitively. If you are consumed with anger, you will constantly receive situations and people in your life that add fuel to the fire of anger. It's as if you are constantly asking the Universe to keep you angry all of the time...*because you are.* By dwelling on your anger consistently and with emotion, you are asking the Universe to give you more anger. If you constantly say to yourself, "I don't want to be angry any more," that's what you will get. The Universe doesn't hear "I don't want to be..."; it only hears the word *angry.* The law of attraction doesn't compute *don't,* *not* or *no,* or any other words of negation. As you speak words of negation, this is what the law of attraction is receiving:

"I don't want to be angry any more."
The Universe hears: *I want to be angry.*

"I don't want to be sick any more."
The Universe hears: *I want to be sick.*

"I don't want to have any more episodes."
The Universe hears: *I want to have episodes.*

"I don't want to fight with my spouse any more."
The Universe hears: *I want to fight with my spouse.*

"I don't want to be in debt again."
The Universe hears: *I want to be in debt again.*

"I don't want to go back into the hospital."
The Universe hears: *I want to go back into the hospital.*

Why doesn't the Universe hear the words *not, no,* or *don't?* It's because you are focused on the thoughts and the ideas of what you don't want. Because you are giving energy, thought and focus to these negative ideas, you are giving them life. If you could change your thoughts from "I don't want to be angry any more" to "I want to be joyful," you would be shifting your thoughts from a focus on negative outcomes to a focus asking for and anticipating positive outcomes.

Plain and simple, we get mad because things don't work out the way we want them to and we don't get our way. What we don't understand is that we *are* getting our own way. We're getting exactly what we're asking for because we are focusing our thoughts on negative ideas. If we could correct our thought processes, we could begin to receive what we truly want. And if we received what we truly wanted, would we have reasons to be angry any more? If we corrected our negative thought patterns and included gratitude in that process, we could change our entire lives. It's very difficult to be grateful and angry at the same time. It's also hard to be grateful and selfish at the same time.

Human beings are funny—they all think everyone should be focused on them and their individual lives. It's kind of like being a teenager all over again. We are all convinced that everyone is interested and consumed with what we do every moment of the day, when that is simply not true. Self-centeredness is the best way to stay angry. You have to stop letting negative emotions and thoughts control your life. You can be bitter or better, but you cannot be both. It is about time you made the decision to conquer your anger and go on to live life.

ANXIETY

Do not be anxious about anything, but in everything, by prayer and petition, with thanksgiving, present your request to God. And the peace of God, which transcends all understanding, will guard your hearts and your minds in Christ Jesus.

—Philippians 4:6-7 NIV

I realize that some anxiety comes from a biochemical origin, but a lot of the anxiety that we feel is self-imposed. Some anxiety begins in our emotions, not our minds. Some people live in a constant state of turmoil and fear. These types of people have a tendency to embroil everyone around them in the fires of their latest anticipated catastrophe, real or imagined. The more you are around these people, the more anxious *you* feel. All of us have enough anxiety, biochemical or emotional, in our lives. No one needs any more.

Let's clarify the difference between concern and anxiety. Concern involves wanting to see things done well so that God receives glory from our lives. Concern is productive. It is forward-looking and positive. Anxiety is the opposite—it is counterproductive, stuck in the present and negative. Concern motivates us to take action. Anxiety paralyzes us.

The best way to figure out what is causing your anxiety is to simply list what makes you anxious. Here are some of the top ones I hear from my clients:

- deep hurts from the past
- lack of self-worth
- desire for total control
- concern for what others think
- striving to "keep up with the Joneses"
- living in "the tomorrow"
- traffic
- crowds

- holidays

- trying to get others to change to meet our needs

- loss of a job

- finding a doctor

- thinking about the future

- day to day tasks

- lust for things we want

- disappointment

- emotions controlling us

Of course, this is not a complete tabulation of everything that might cause anxiety. But, I'm sure, you could find at least three or four things that might apply to your life.

Here's the good news—you don't have to feel anxious and nervous all of the time about anything in your life. God promises us in Philippians 4:6-7 that if we give Him all of our anxiety, He'll give us peace. And He makes good on His promises, whether you have bipolar disorder or not. I cannot begin to tell you how many times I have had to call upon the Lord to help me with my self-imposed anxiety.

> *Humble yourselves, therefore, under God's mighty hand, that He may lift you up in due time. Cast all your anxiety on Him because He cares for you.*
>
> —1 Peter 5:6-7 NIV

CHAPTER 6 — FAITH

The next time you are feeling anxiety starting to take control, try these suggestions:

- Refuse to allow anxiety to become a "state of being" in your life.

- Believe God when He says you are worthy of His constant care.

- Yield total control of every area of your life to God.

- Refuse to be caught up in what others think of you.

- Refuse to be trapped into operating according to the "world's" standards of "success."

- Get your priorities in line with God's priorities for you.

- Choose to live in today, not tomorrow.

> *But seek first His kingdom and His righteousness, and all these things will be given to you as well. Therefore, do not worry about tomorrow, for tomorrow will worry about itself. Each day has enough trouble of its own.*
>
> —Matthew 6:33, 34 NIV

Here's a prayer from Charles Stanley, pastor and author, to help you deal with your own anxiety.

"Say to the Lord, 'You are in control of this situation. I trust You to deal with this troublesome person or persons, or these circumstances. Help me to give my full attention to the task that You have put in front of me right now. Calm my heart, focus my attention, infuse my mind with Your ideas and creative solutions, and give me the strength to be diligent until this project or meeting is completed.'"

Size means nothing to God. What is impossible for us is nothing for Him. You've got to stop looking at situations, people and illnesses through your own eyes and realize that your viewpoint is not His viewpoint.

Trusting God is a scary proposition. For most of our lives, we've put our faith and trust in other people and they've let us down. So why should it be any easier when it comes to God? Here's why: if you have a relationship with Jesus, God promises He will always be there for us. As I said before, He always makes good on His promises. This success formula does not come from me—it is directly from God.

You have the control over what you dwell upon. Every person has the ability to say, "I will think about something else," or "I will think about this in a different way." Then you have the ability to do just that: refocus your mind on a different subject or task, or reframe your thoughts to a more positive slant. You just have to make the choice to step out and believe in His promise, and your life will improve and your anxiety lessen because He's in control now...and trust me, He manages my life much better than I ever could!

FEAR

> *God has not given us a spirit of fear, but of power, and of love and of a sound mind.*
>
> —2 Timothy 1:7

How many times have you allowed fear to dictate what happens in your life? Have you ever sat down and wondered what you are actually afraid of and why? I remember when I used to let fear control me. I was always worried about my next episode, people finding out that I had bipolar disorder, not being accepted or loved because of my disorder, losing my job and/or the stigma that surrounds having a psychological disorder.

Fear clouds the mind, stifles thinking and snuffs out creativity. It causes tension in the body, which often leads to temporary emotional paralysis or a failure to act. Fear weakens our confidence and boldness, keeping us from praying and reaching the full potential that God has for us in every area of our lives.

Way too many of us are not living our dreams because we are living our fears. Fear does not have any special power unless we empower it with our thoughts. We see what makes us fearful rather than what makes us safe. You will become whatever your fear tells you if you let it. You choose to side with fear.

I realized that there are two paths you can take in life. You can view life as a series of problems, fears, and failures or you can see life as a series of experiences, opportunities, and adventures. It is **exactly** the same life. It's just that the perspective is different. You are the one who chooses the perspective. **The choice is always yours.**

Here's a little story to illustrate my point. Peter was one of Jesus' rowdiest disciples. He was always putting his foot in his mouth, saying exactly what was on his mind and doing the wrong things at the wrong time. I always related to Peter so well because I'm the same way—always saying what is on my mind, politically correct or not. The cool thing about Peter was the fact that Jesus loved him simply because he was never lukewarm in his thoughts, speech or actions.

One night, the disciples were all in a boat on the lake. One of the disciples noticed that there was a figure moving across the water. At first, they all thought it was a ghost and they cried out in fear, but Jesus immediately said to them, "Take courage, it is I. Don't be afraid." Peter, being the one who always spoke before he thought, said, "Lord, if it's you, tell me to come to you on the water." Then Peter got down out of the boat and *walked on the water* and came toward Jesus. What part of walking on the water did Peter not notice? He was so focused on reaching Jesus that he didn't even acknowledge his fear, nor did he notice he was in water deep enough to drown. But then, he took his eyes off the goal—reaching Jesus. All of a sudden, he noticed the wind and the water and he began to sink. He cried out, "Lord, save me." Immediately, Jesus reached out his hand and caught him. Jesus said, "Ye of little faith, why did you doubt?" Amazing story, isn't it?

Peter had enough faith to take action even though he was filled with fear. He was focused enough, even if only for a short time, to perform a miraculous feat: walking on water. Unfortunately, many of us never face the fear or focus in faith long enough to even get out of the boat, let alone try to walk on the water.

One of the fears I hear potential clients express quite frequently is the fear of discontinuing ineffective medications in favor of trying more effective treatments. Even though their lives are much worse, at times, due to taking these medications, they stubbornly refuse to look at other options, even when I have presented them with qualified research about integrative treatments, given them other positive client testimonials from people who have been through the same process and given them trusted, board-certified doctor referrals they can consult. Why would people refuse to try a better way? One word: *fear.*

I, too, was afraid of discontinuing medication. From the very first day I was diagnosed, I was told that I would never be able to live my life free of medication. Even though each new medication seemed to make me feel worse, I'd bought into the belief that medication was the answer. I was taking medication for the side effects of other medication. For an active person like myself, it didn't make sense to take all of these medications that made me feel progressively physically, emotionally and mentally worse off than I was before diagnosis. This fear cost me about six years of my life, two of which I barely remember because I was so medicated.

Finally, I was given an overdose of medication which caused me to have a seizure. While I was lying in the hospital bed, it dawned on me that my fear was killing me—literally. I had known what the right path for me to take was, the whole time. But I was afraid. As I started to take each new medication, I knew in my gut that this path was wrong for me. Yet, I continued to allow all of the external forces to control decisions about *my* body, *my* mind, *my* brain. Why? Because I was afraid. I was afraid to trust myself and do what I felt was right for me to do.

So, what did I do with my fear? I made a decision. I took action. It's that simple. Difficult decisions are always that way. **It's never easy, but it's always simple.**

I decided while in the hospital to find a better way to treat my illness that didn't make me sicker and would allow me to live the life that I wanted.

So, here I am, six years later, helping other people to face their fears, make decisions and take action. The Lord led me to the doctor who helped me safely transition off my medications with a minimal risk to myself.

I no longer take psychiatric medications and have experienced no symptoms and no episodes in four years. Am I glad I faced my fear? Absolutely. Otherwise, I'd still be trapped in a prison of medication today. I might not have lived to survive other seizures and/or medication side effects.

Now, if you happen to be tired of being afraid all of the time, here's the solution God has laid out for us and that I follow to face my fears—stop trusting yourself and trust God. You are right; you do not have the power to control all of the things that will happen to you on a daily basis. But God does. God is still in control. **The quickest way to stop fear is faith.**

Much of fear is rooted in doubt that God will be present, provide justice and help or be capable of dealing with the crisis at hand. Faith says, "Yes, God is here. Yes, God will provide. Yes, God is capable of all things!"

STRESS

> *And being in anguish, He prayed more earnestly, and his sweat was like drops of blood falling to the ground.*
>
> —Luke 22:44 NIV

I doubt if any of us has been as stressed out as Jesus was in the above scripture. Scientists have shown that this "sweating drops of blood" is an actual physiological possibility brought on by—you guessed it—stress!

The leading cause of physical illness in the United States right now is stress. We've all noticed that heart disease, cancer, autoimmune deficiency illness and hormonal imbalances are all on the rise. These illnesses are killing people at an alarming rate, and most of the root cause of these illnesses can be traced back to stress.

Most of us are stressed because we don't know the outcome of "whatever"—what our days, months, years, and lives will hold for us. I'm sure everyone would like to have a crystal ball at home that would foretell the future. Here's the problem with that: it would probably frighten us tremendously.

We believe it is up to us to make things right, and we always want to be in charge of everything. But unless you're from the planet Krypton, you ain't Superman! Our lives evolve quickly on a daily basis, and a lot of the stress that we feel comes from that change and our lack of control over that change. It all comes back to us not being able to control every single thing that involves our lives.

You have to finally come to a point where you accept that God loves you, He knows where you are every second of every day and He is bigger than any problem life's circumstances can throw at you. You have to have complete confidence that God is able to take care of any situation and that He will provide an answer to any question or problem. He has all the resources of the universe to draw upon in helping each one of us through any type of crisis if we will just trust Him.

If you haven't figured it out yet, we cannot control our lives. Only God can. I hate to keep beating a dead horse, but it always comes back to trusting God with our lives. He loves us more than any human could ever love us and wants nothing but the best for us. If you will surrender your control, you will feel a massive weight come off your shoulders. God promises that if we give up "the good" of controlling our own lives, He will deliver "the great" of a new life with Him in control.

PEACE

> Peace I leave with you; my peace I give you. I do not give to you as the world gives. Do not let your hearts be troubled and do not be afraid.
>
> —John 14:27 NIV

Have you ever wanted to lie down and feel nothing but perfect peace? Most of the time, our thoughts are racing so fast and our anxiety is so high that peace seems more like a fantasy than a reality. The peace that you have found to be so evasive can be yours. God tells us in Matthew 11:28–30, "Come to me, all you who are weary and burdened,

CHAPTER 6 — FAITH

I will give you rest. Take my yoke upon you and learn of me, for I am gentle and humble of heart and you will find rest for your souls. For my yoke is easy and my burden is light." Is this just too easy for us to embrace and live every day?

I've never met a person who woke up one morning and said, "I think I'd like to live in stress and chaos, and have my whole world collapse around me today." Although there seem to be some people who enjoy living in the middle of chaos, most of us don't seek that kind of life. We do not seek turmoil. At one time or another, I'm sure most of us have heard someone say, "Could I just get some peace around here?" The cry of our hearts is not for just a moment of peace, but for a lifetime of peace.

Peace is an inner quality that flows out of a right relationship with God. Why do I keep talking so much about trusting God and having a relationship with Him? Perhaps I can answer that by illustrating what happens when you don't trust God as the one in control of your life....

- If you're controlled by the particular situation you are facing, you can't have peace because at any second that situation can spin out of control. Life's circumstances can change in a heartbeat.

- If some evil power is in control, you are certainly in trouble. (In today's world of terrorism, this one is scary to contemplate!)

- If another person controls you or the circumstance in which you are involved, you may have peace for a while, but eventually that person will disappoint you and let you down in some way, and you can lose your peace.

- If you are in control, you may appear to have the power to guarantee yourself a peaceful existence, but eventually you are going to make a mistake or something or someone will enter the picture to rearrange your circumstances. Then you will find your ability to create and control your own serenity was a mere illusion.

But what if God is in control of your life? With Him guiding your life, there's every reason to hope, every reason to feel confident and every reason to move forward boldly in your life, expecting the best out of every experience. He's the expert on your life. He made you. He formed you. He knows every part of your being better than you do. He's all knowing and all-powerful, and He's the perfect being to run your life.

You cannot have peace and at the same time have doubt that God will provide for you. Focus your work on those things God has put in your path to do, and help others to the best of your ability. God has ways and means of providing for you that you haven't even dreamed about. Again, you cannot have peace and at the same time have doubt that God will provide for you. Settle the issue once and for all in your heart and mind. God is your Provider. In this knowledge and belief, you will find peace.

HOPE

I have told you these things, so that in me you may have peace. In this world you will have trouble. But take heart! I have overcome the world.

—John 16:33 NIV

I know what it feels like to live a life completely devoid of any hope. I know the darkness that the illness brings. I've lined the pills up, I've made the phone calls to friends to say goodbye. I know what it feels like to say to myself and to others, "I just can't take the pain any more." So why didn't I do it? What kept me going?

When I accepted Christ in 1986, He promised me hope. And somewhere in the back of my mind, I clung to that promise. I knew that somehow, some way, things in my life would get better if I could just hold on for a little while longer.

Today, I know that the Scripture above is true. Christ has truly overcome the world—the world of fear, anxiety, sickness, doubt, stress, emotional instability—all of the challenges that threatened to destroy me.

At some point, you have to make a decision to fully trust God and believe His promises. Had I not believed His promises, I wouldn't be here today to write this book. I would have ended my life because I couldn't face the pain by myself any more. I couldn't see any answers because I was looking at the world from my viewpoint, not God's.

Christ is the wellspring of hope and joy. He is the promise that tomorrow will be a better day. He is the promise that even though we can't see a way out of our troubles, He can. Joy is forever as long as we keep our eyes on Him. He is my source of continued hope.

That being said, one of the things that troubles me the most about the psychological community is the lack of hope that is given to those who are diagnosed with bipolar disorder. All of the focus is on the horrible symptoms, story after story of gloom and doom and how people are relegated to living lives medicated to the hilt with no prospects of ever improving. They are taken from jobs of responsibility and moved to menial, demeaning hourly positions simply because they cannot function on all of the medications they are taking. Web site after web site spends pages and pages on horror stories about destroyed lives, limitations placed on people who have bipolar disorder and wasted human potential.

I'm here to say, "Wake up!" There are people like myself living fully, productively, successfully and happily. There is hope. There are answers. If you have to have bipolar disorder, this is the absolute best time in history to have it. Consider what would have happened to you had you lived in the Dark Ages with this illness. You would have probably been burnt at the stake. Even just forty years ago, you would have probably been institutionalized for life. Technology and its impact on the medical field is changing every day.

My pastor recently said, **"Don't lie down until they put you down."** In other words, don't give up—there's still hope. Look at my life. Go back and read the introduction of this book again. I was told to give up my life and go on disability. But I clung to the hope that I could find a successful way to manage bipolar disorder. I did, and you are reading it.

Success Summary

- Jesus can change your life.

- God doesn't "play dice."

- God will show you your purpose if you ask Him.

- Self-centeredness is the best way to stay angry.

- If you give God control of your life, your anxiety will lessen.

- God did not give us the spirit of fear.

- Stress is the leading cause of physical illness in the United States.

- Stop worrying about the past and the future, and focus on today!

- God promises to give us peace if we ask for it.

- If you let God have control of your life, you can relax and lose your anxiety and fear.

- Christ has overcome the world—never give up hope!

CHAPTER 7
Winning

Far better is it to dare mighty things, to win glorious triumphs even though checkered by failure, than to rank with those poor spirits who neither enjoy nor suffer much because they live in the grey twilight that knows neither victory nor defeat.

—Theodore Roosevelt

WINNING

The reason I call this last chapter "Winning" is because winning the battle against bipolar disorder has been my focus for the last four years, and I hope that you see now that it really is possible for you to win this battle as well. I have lived the last four years successfully, and I have no doubt that I will live the rest of my life victorious against this illness.

Throughout all of my years of coaching basketball, I never allowed myself or my players to believe that anything but victory was ever possible. I remember I had a group of kids one year that had gone 0-12 their previous season. Self-confidence wasn't really a problem—because they didn't have any! I had to spend the summer and the first several weeks of practice convincing these kids that they were winners. When the season started, we won our first game and I could see them start to believe in themselves again. We went on to win the next seven games before we experienced our first loss. It was astounding to watch the kids just stand on the floor after the final buzzer of the ninth game in total shock because we had lost. It was amazing because this same group of kids six months earlier didn't believe that they could win. That final game, with an 8-0 start, they didn't think they could lose.

My goal as those kids' coach wasn't just to equip them for sports—it was to equip them for life. If my players believed that they could never lose, they would be unstoppable in their everyday lives and would go on to accomplish and achieve great things.

You have got to believe that you cannot lose.

WE'VE GOT THEM RIGHT
WHERE WE WANT THEM

Here's a great example of what perception, attitude and a desire to succeed can do for you. Several years ago, I was coaching a girls' basketball team in the State games. It was about four to five minutes into the game and we had failed to even get the ball past half-court. I mean, we were gettin' whooped by at least seventeen to twenty points. I remember standing there and thinking, "If I don't do something quick, this is going to get very embarrassing; we might as well go ahead and get on the bus and save ourselves the pain." So, during our next possession, I called a time out. I knew that the kids were thinking as they ran to the huddle that I was getting ready to let them have it about how sorry they were playing. Instead, I figured I'd try a little reverse psychology and see what happened.

So I knelt down in the huddle, looked at the kids and said, "Okay, we've got 'em right where we want 'em!"

Dead silence.

I will never forget the look on my assistant coach's face. He was in total shock. They all looked at me as if I had lost my mind.

I proceeded to tell the kids that the other team was extremely overconfident, that this was the moment to come back and exactly how we were going to do it. When the horn blew and it was time for us to go back out onto the floor, I could tell by the look in those kids' eyes that they actually believed what I said. They knew that there was no way we were going to lose that game. A different team walked on that court and we went on to win by twenty points.

So, what changed? Was it the kids or the kids' perception of what was really happening? It just goes to show you how much your attitude and your viewpoint play into whether you succeed or fail.

> *Many dream but few dream and then fulfill.*
>
> —Paul J. Meyer

Throughout the book I've discussed finding what you truly want, forming the right attitude, creating your effective treatment team, why nutrition is the cornerstone of success, the critical impact exercise has on your illness and how a relationship with God can provide purpose, hope and meaning for your life. Now, here is how you put it all together...

GOALS

Goals are the blueprints for making your dreams come true. Remember, there is more to building a house successfully than just a set of blueprints, but this is where we'll start.

Let's clarify the difference between goals and dreams. Goals are the measurements of our actions. They generally don't involve feeling or emotion. They are simply milestones on the path of life for us to use as measures of our "success." They are checkmarks on life's "To Do" list.

Goals must be written, realistic, specific, measurable and consistent with your values. My goal was to live an episode-free life. From that goal, I then outlined what I would have to do to achieve it. For you, this is going to be a whole lot easier! By using this book, you can quickly "cut to the chase," take this action plan, apply it to your life and personalize the plan with your own goals. I am saving you the time, the pain and the money of having to go through all of the painful (and costly) experiences that I had to endure.

But let's walk through the steps, just to make sure you have gotten your money's worth! Everything, and I do mean *everything,* that I have put into this book, I have put into place in my own life. Just like in Chapter 1, I had to physically sit down and write out what I really wanted. Just in case you were wondering, these are the things I really wanted:

- the same winning attitude toward my illness that I had on the basketball court

- a medical team that would challenge the traditional approach of medication and talk therapy and would treat me from a body-mind-soul perspective

- a nutrition plan that would be the cornerstone of a proactive approach to my illness

- an exercise program that would give me a strong body, but also a strong mind

- an ever-increasing faith in Christ that would give me a worry-free life filled with hope, peace and joy

Guess what, folks? I have achieved every one of those desires through establishing clear and specific goals. This book is even one of the many by-products that have originated from my first goals. Goals are always evolving and ever changing—if you are accomplishing them!

Now remember, none of the stuff that I've just covered means anything unless you write your goals down. No exceptions. The fastest way to achieve your goals is to rewrite them every single day. Studies have shown that people who write their goals every day are one hundred times more likely to achieve them than people who do not. **Writing down your goals every day allows you to stay focused and keeps you from trading what you want for what you want right now.** For more information on goal setting, go to www.jackcanfield.com under the heading "Media Room," select "Articles for Reprint" and read the article "How to Program Your Mind."

BABY STEPS

I don't know what your goals are or will be. Some goals could be to reduce your medications, find a doctor that listens, get the weight off that was caused by the side effects of your medicine or get a job you enjoy where you can use your talents and creativity. Right now, your biggest goal may be to just simply get out of bed each day. I remember some days when getting out of bed was the equivalent of climbing Mount Everest. You lie in bed and wonder who came in during the night and sucked all of the life out of you. You bargain with yourself that you will get up in just a minute, you keep bargaining and before you know it, four or five hours have passed by and you are still lying there trying to talk yourself out of bed.

Everything has to be done in baby steps. Your goal may be to get out of bed every morning at eight A.M. Give yourself two or three objectives that help you meet your goal.

- Develop a "relaxation routine" that will help prepare you for sleep one hour before bedtime (meditation, warm glass of milk, herbal tea, reading, prayer—whatever works for you!).

- Go to bed at an established time (nine or ten P.M.).

- Utilize a "sleep system" alarm that works with your brain waves or a computer-based, voice-activated system that uses a soothing voice to awaken you without startling you.

- Set up a reward system for getting out of bed on time—the task must be performed five days straight before you receive your reward.

A good way to start the goal-setting process is to set a goal to do "X" within a thirty days. If you want to test this theory, a simple goal you can set would be to walk for twenty minutes, five days a week for thirty days. This is a reasonable goal because it doesn't cost any money, require any equipment or require a trip to the gym, and it increases your metabolic rate and improves your overall health. This one goal, as simple as it is, will improve your energy and mood level, allow you to lose weight, get you some much needed fresh air and sunlight—and who knows, you may meet some really nice neighbors in the process.

PAY THE PRICE

You have to be willing to pay the price for attaining your goals. Nothing is free. Whatever you are aiming at, stick with it! The right habits and attitudes are required before any goal can be achieved. In other words, you must be prepared to change as a person before any tangible results will appear.

PASSION AND DESIRE

Desire is more important than talent, race, intellect, looks, degrees or background. When I was coaching, I would pick a kid who had desire over a kid who had talent any day of the week. A kid who has talent but no desire is like a cancer on the team. A player with desire always gives it everything he has and raises the overall intensity of the team. Several years ago, I was coaching a team with two kids that fit the "desire level" I was looking for. Their names were Ryan and Chris. By no means were these the two the most talented kids I ever coached, but nobody could out-work them or out-hustle them. That made them indispensable to my basketball team.

Passion and desire are not something I can teach on the basketball court or in this book. It is something that must be born within you, something that resonates within your soul. You must be able to tap into this power. Passion almost creates superhuman ability. Everyone has this power. You just have to find out what activates and fuels a passion so strong nothing can stop it.

My passion was fueled by the memory of Robby Murray. Robby played for me and was killed in a car accident when he was fifteen. Every day at practice, I used to talk to Robby about passion and the fact that he had to work hard and never give up, regardless of the circumstances. Now, any time I feel like giving up, I know that quitting is just not an option because I have to demand from myself everything I demanded from Robby.

If you add passion and desire to a specific goal and plan, you are virtually unstoppable. You'll be on a crusade for success.

> *A dream, backed up by a crusade is an almost unstoppable combination. Crusaders die hard.*
>
> —Art Williams

4 STAGES OF DESIRE

- Desire gains strength when it has a concrete form. Goal setting forces you to decide *exactly* what your dream is.

- Desire becomes obsession.

- Desire becomes commitment.

- Desire becomes endurance.

> *Desire is the ingredient that causes people to devote their lives to a dream and keep moving toward it, no matter what!*
>
> —Art Williams

PROACTIVE, NOT REACTIVE

> *I teach people to overcome things before they ever happen.*
>
> —Scot Ferrell

It seems like everywhere you go in life, people operate in the "Chicken Little" syndrome. Remember him? He's the one who always ran around saying, "The sky is falling, the sky is falling!" even when there was really nothing wrong. This chick reacted negatively to everything! I know as you sit here reading this, a situation has come to your mind that matches this scenario. Maybe that situation is a traffic jam. How many reactions do the "stupid drivers" get out of you every time you get stuck in traffic? I know you're sitting there screaming obscenities at the guy in the yellow convertible who just swerved in front of you. Did your reaction have any effect on his life or his mood? Of course not. However, it did dictate what frame of mind you would be in, maybe for the rest of the day.

I hear stories from the educational systems, support groups and Corporate America all the time about how hours and hours and hours are spent dwelling on every little intimate detail about what's wrong with a situation. And yet, how very little time is spent on strategies to actually correct the problems! I remember countless meetings, conferences, in-services and "consultations" about what my problems were, but nobody ever offered productive solutions. There were always ideas that were discussed ad nauseam, but they were never logistically practical, were totally devoid of common sense and were usually a re-hash of the process we already had in place that didn't work. For some reason, people love to dwell on the negative. Well, the buck stops here.

We are all familiar with the problems that accompany having bipolar disorder. Isn't it about time to actually fix the problem before it ever starts? All of us need a system in place to manage any and all problems before they take place. So, here's what I need you to do: write a plan. This plan should cover the following contingencies:

- what to do to prevent a manic episode

- what to do if a manic episode occurs

- what to do to prevent a depressive episode

- what to do if a depressive episode occurs

- what to do to prevent financial crises

- what to do if a financial crises arises

- management of your legal affairs if you are incapacitated

- lists of supplements, medications, doctors' contact information and anyone or anything else connected to your medical team (I wear a Medic Alert bracelet because I have a fatal allergy to certain medicines)

- lists of credit cards, bank accounts and insurance information (i.e. photocopies of cards) stored in a safe place that is easily accessible

I discovered years ago, it is much easier to live life preventing manic and depressive episodes than dealing with the consequences of reacting to the episodes. When I instruct my clients to make these lists, I make sure that they have the appropriate people involved in the process. These could be your wife, your parents, your best friends, your roommate or your pastor. Every detail of the plan must be agreed upon by the entire "committee," signed and dated. It is also important to keep these plans and lists updated as changes occur. This plan takes all the emotion out of dealing with every situation and allows you or the "committee" to deal with just the facts. This gives everybody peace of mind and alleviates a lot of the stress that comes with having an illness.

NO MORE NEGATIVES!

"Security is mostly a superstition. It does not exist in nature....Life is either a daring adventure or nothing."

—Helen Keller

Dealing with this illness is hard enough without having to deal with all the negatives that surround us on a daily basis. You have to deal with your own negative thoughts, negative loved ones, a negative job or boss, negative physical symptoms, negative societal reactions and negative reactions to medications—you name it. If it is negative, we have to deal with it!

So, what did I do? I had to take a hard look at my life and what surrounded and influenced me on a daily basis. I sat down, made a list of all my friends and listed whether they had a positive or negative influence on my life. If they had a negative influence on my life, I stopped hanging around them. All they were going to do was stop me from achieving the success that I wanted to accomplish. We all have that "one friend" who has the black cloud that follows him around, and he doesn't mind if his cloud rains on you! After I made this list, I made another one that outlined the positives and negatives of my job, my health, my doctors, my business associates, my church, my family, my dating partners, my hobbies and anything that occurred in my life. I then reviewed this list, and if the negatives of one category outweighed the positives, I eliminated that from my life.

As I always love to say, **"This is simple...not easy."** On paper, it is very obvious and clear-cut which things and people need to leave your life. However, when it comes to the emotional part of doing it, things get much tougher. You have to remember: your life up to today is your comfort zone, and it is painful to get outside your comfort zone. But if you want to be successful, you do not have any choice. Let me repeat.... **If you want to be successful, you do not have any choice. No matter how hard you work to create and maintain positive thoughts, energy and excitement, if you are constantly surrounded by negative people, they will suck the joy right out of your life—whether you have bipolar disorder or not!**

WHAT YOU SEE IS WHAT YOU GET

Remember back in Chapter 1, I asked you to write down what you really want in life? By now, you have written it down, but have you begun to visualize what your life would be like if what was on the paper materialized in your life? It's true, what you see in your mind is what will materialize in your everyday life. What you see is what you get! I spend at least ten to fifteen minutes per day visualizing all my goals and my dreams and how I want them to materialize in my life.

As I step into my new midnight blue car, I catch a whiff of the "fine Corinthian leather" as the seat contours itself around my body as if to say, "Welcome home, Scot!" I crank that baby up, put it in gear, and take off. Then, I pop in some Metallica and feel the beat begin as my heart starts to pound with the bass drums. My car's interior becomes my own private Utopia where I am lord and master and tranquility rules (and there is no traffic!) I feel peaceful and powerful because I am in my kingdom where I rule and reign supremely!

Did you realize that I do not even own this car yet? Could you feel how vivid my visualization is? What you see is what you get. Every one of my dreams is visualized to this extent and I have no doubt that they will all come true...because thoughts become things and your subconscious mind cannot tell the difference between reality and fantasy.

I was fortunate enough to have a friend that introduced me to a film called *The Secret*. This film has the power to change lives. It will transform your life immediately. It will make visualization more clear to you and will show you how *every thought* you have influences everything in your life. Go to www.thesecret.tv for more information. Do this immediately!

GRATITUDE AND LAUGHTER

The way I start every day is by sharing with God how grateful I am for everything in my life. I realize I have bipolar disorder, but I *could* have had XXXX (you fill in the blank). When you have an "attitude of gratitude," it begins to focus your attention away from the negative things in your life and gives energy to the positive thoughts you are expressing. The law of attraction states that you will attract whatever you are thinking and feeling. So if you constantly focus on how bad you feel, how unfair life is and how mean people are, you will constantly be attracting that to you. On the flip side, if you consistently focus and feel positive toward your life—and yes, even your illness—you will be amazed at how positive things start to flow into your life. It all starts with a feeling of gratitude for what you have now and for what you will have in the future.

When you are writing your goals, write them in a manner that reflects gratitude. For example, *I am grateful and happy that I have a healthy mind, a strong body and a loving relationship with my husband.* Always write things in "the now" instead of in the past or future. *The Secret* will help you with this also.

You have always heard that "laughter is the best medicine." Well, it's true! I make sure I laugh as much as I can every day. Laughter has an amazing healing power. The movie *Patch Adams* (with Robin Williams) is a great example of this. Watch funny movies, tell jokes with your kids and do whatever it takes to bring on a good belly laugh. Make this a conscious effort on your part. Start with smiling at everyone you pass, whether they return the smile or not. When you smile at someone else, you make them feel better, and in turn you feel better, and in turn others around you feel better and on and on and on.... People are attracted to people who make them laugh. So now would be a good time to give this a shot; it's probably the easiest thing you can do to improve your mood and your day!

DON'T EVER QUIT!

Quitting is easy. Anybody can quit. In fact, most people do. If you quit, your opportunity to achieve your dreams is lost. I know what it's like to start a suicide note; I have lined up the pills on my bathroom counter, deciding which ones to take, and called my friends to tell them goodbye and that I can't take it anymore. No one knows better than I do how hard dealing with bipolar disorder and all of its madness is.

The funny thing is, I now am accused of not knowing what it would be like to have depression and bipolar disorder. Sometimes, people in support groups look and listen to me and assume that I have never dealt with the "dark sides" of bipolar disorder. People do not realize how many years it has taken for me to do the work that had to be done in order for me to now be successful. How many times do you hear people say, "Well, if I had a golf swing like Tiger Woods, of course I could make all of that money!" Do you have any idea how many years, months, weeks, days and hours Tiger Woods has practiced with no one watching to become what he is today?

So this is what I am asking you to do. Make a commitment. Write down the commitment. Write down the price you are going to have to pay, and accept that you can be successful if you are willing to do **whatever it takes to achieve your success!**

It is no use saying, "We are doing our best." You have got to succeed in doing what is necessary.

—Sir Winston Churchill

As a coach, I never accepted defeat. And because of that attitude, I never had to experience it very often. I never worried about the other team very much because I knew if we did what we knew how to do and gave the game everything we had, we would emerge victorious. I never allowed my players to even consider losing. If you are a winner, losing is never an option. **Success is the only option.**

Over the course of this book, I have outlined for you what it takes to win against bipolar disorder. Now it's your job to decide the outcome of the game. I have a wonderful life, and I can promise you that whatever price you pay, a wonderful life is worth it. I get up every day and thank God that I didn't quit, give up my dreams, and go on disability like my former doctor suggested. I am in the process of fulfilling all my dreams, and I get excited every morning when I get up and think about all the wonderful things that are yet to come in my life. You see, I am a success, and nothing can stop me from achieving anything that my mind can conceive.

Now, get up. Go look in the mirror and tell the person you are looking at that you're going to win and be a success. The person looking back at you will be the only person who can ever beat you in life. It is time to conquer that person. **You will become successful over bipolar disorder just like I am. Now, you have the tools. Go claim your success!**

Success Summary

- You have got to believe that you cannot lose!

- Many dream, but few dream and then fulfill.

- Goals must be written, realistic, specific, measurable and consistent with your values.

- Remember that you need to take baby steps.

- You have to be willing to pay the price for obtaining your goals—nothing is free!

- Desire is more important than talent, race, intellect, looks, degrees or background.

- A dream backed up by a crusade is an almost unstoppable combination.

- There are four stages of desire: goal setting, obsession, commitment and endurance.

- Be proactive, not reactive!

- Write a crisis prevention plan.

- No more negatives!

- Remember, this is simple...not easy!

- What you see is what you get! You must visualize your goals and dreams.

- Always include gratitude and laughter in your every day life.

- Don't ever quit!

- You are a winner! Don't ever let the person in the mirror stop you!

- Victory is the only option!

INDEX

ATTITUDE INVENTORY

Below is a survey that I ask all of my clients to fill out when I begin to mentor them. You can use this to help further investigate your current attitude as discussed in Chapter 2.

1) How did you feel about your future before you were diagnosed?

2) How did you feel about your future after you were diagnosed?

3) How do you feel about your future now?

4) On a scale of 1 to 10, with 1 being the worst and 10 being the best, what is your quality of life right now?

5) If you could describe your perfect life, what would it look like?

6) If you were to say that you were managing your bipolar disorder successfully, what exactly would that mean to you?

Primary Neurotransmitter Depletion Diseases

Parkinsonism	Chronic fatigue syndrome	Adrenal fatigue/burnout
Obesity	Bulimia	Hyperactivity
Anorexia	ADHD/ADD	Depression
Anxiety	Hormone dysfunction	Adrenal dysfunction
Panic Attacks	Migraine headaches	Dementia
Phobias	Tension headaches	Alzheimer's disease
Impulsivity	Traumatic brain injury	Premenstrual syndrome
Chronic Pain	Menopausal symptoms	Nocturnal Myoclonus
Obsessionality	Crohn's disease	Obsessive compulsive
Insomnia	Irritable bowel syndrome	Ulcerative colitis
Fibromyalgia	Inappropriate aggression	Inappropriate anger
Psychotic illness	Cognitive deterioration	Cortisol dysfunction
Management of chronic stress	Organ system dysfunction	

SUGGESTED READING

Ageless: The Naked Truth About Bioidentical Hormones
> Suzanne Somers
>
> www.suzannesomers.com

Unlocking Your Legacy
> Paul J. Meyer

Natural Cures
> Kevin Trudeau
>
> www.naturalcures.com

Now, Discover Your Strengths
> Marcus Buckingham & Donald Clifton
>
> www.strengthsfinder.com

The Lean Body Promise
> Lee Labrada
>
> www.leanbodypromise.com
>
> www.labrada.com

Powerful Medicines: The Benefits, Risks, and Costs of Prescription Drugs

Dr. Jerry Avorn

Brain Trust

Colm Kelleher, Ph.D.

Depression-Free for Life

Dr. Gabriel Cousens, M.D.

www.treeoflife.nu

Be Anxious For Nothing

Joyce Meyer

www.joycemeyer.org

Finding Peace

Charles Stanley

The Secret

Rhonda Byrne

www.thesecret.tv

SUGGESTED PRODUCTS

Aloe Products

www.lqintl.com

I take a juice (LiquiVida) and a capsule form (MVM) of this product.

Energy Drinks

www.quixtar.com

These are the only energy drinks I consume. They consist mostly of B vitamins.

Nutritional Supplements

www.labrada.com

These are the products I personally use; I believe them to be the best on the market.

SUGGESTED RESOURCES

American Holistic Medicine Association
www.holisticmedicine.org
This site also has a physician referral resource on it. You can choose by the specific medical field you are looking for.

Dr. Christine Gustafson, MD
www.gustafsonm-d.com
Alpharetta Integrative Medicine LLC
Dr. Gustafson is my own personal integrative medicine doctor. She is a tremendous resource for me. Her web site is extremely informative about the benefits that an integrative medicine doctor can provide.

Dr. Marion Maloof, D.C.
www.doctormaloof.com
Dr. Maloof is an Atlas Orthogonal chiropractor. He is my personal chiropractor and one of the pioneers of his field. He also has a hyperbaric chamber in his office.

Brian Johnston
www.evolve-now.com
Brian is my personal trainer and nutritionist. His web site offers several options for you in regards to your training needs.

"The Secret"

www.thesecret.tv

This website will allow you to purchase the movie for an immediate download or purchase the DVD of the movie. It will also give you links to all of the "Secret Teachers" who appeared in the movie. I highly recommend that you go to each teacher's web site and review the materials they have available for you to use. Some of the more pertinent teachers I would recommend you to review would be Bob Proctor, James Arthur Ray, John Demartini, David Schirmer, Joe Vitale, John Assaraf, Jack Canfield, Reverend Dr. Michael Beckwith and the "Miracle Man" Morris E. Goodman.

Best Bipolar Tips E-Zine

www.beatbipolartoday.com

This is my own e-zine that includes tips on nutrition, exercise, winning attitudes, success strategies, faith and the latest research regarding bipolar disorder. Once a month, I deliver these directly to you via email. This is a free service I provide for those who want to stay on top of successful bipolar disorder management.

PRAYER OF SALVATION

God wants you to receive His free gift of salvation. Jesus wants to save you and fill you with the Holy Spirit more than anything. If you have never invited Jesus, the Prince of Peace, to be your Lord and Savior, I invite you to do so now. Pray the following prayer, and if you are really sincere about it, you will experience a new life in Christ.

Father,

You loved the world so much, You gave Your only begotten Son to die for our sins so that whoever believes in Him will not perish but have eternal life.

Your Word says we are saved by grace through faith as a gift from You. There is nothing we can do to earn salvation.

I believe and confess with my mouth that Jesus Christ is Your Son, the Savior of the world. I believe He died on the cross for me and bore all of my sins, paying the price for them. I believe in my heart that You raised Jesus from the dead.

I ask You to forgive my sins. I confess Jesus as my Lord. According to Your Word, I am saved and will spend eternity with You! Thank You, Father. I am so grateful. In Jesus' name, Amen.

Printed in the United States
111715LV00002B/238-342/P

9 781599 320533